Contents

1. Introduction to the World of Linux Kernels 1

2. The Genesis of Linux 5
  2.1. A Brief History of Operating Systems 5
  2.2. The Birth of Linux: Ideals and Origins 7
  2.3. Linus Torvalds and the Iconic 'Hello World' 10
  2.4. From Unix to Linux: The Transformation 13
  2.5. Early Challenges in Development 15

3. Understanding the Linux Kernel 19
  3.1. What is a Kernel? 19
  3.2. Key Components: From Scheduler to Memory Management 22
  3.3. Kernel Interfaces and APIs 25
  3.4. Subsystems and Modules Explained 28
  3.5. User Space vs. Kernel Space 32

4. Linux Kernel Architecture 35
  4.1. Monolithic vs. Microkernel Debate 35
  4.2. The Modular Nature of Linux 38
  4.3. The Role of Init Systems 41
  4.4. Boot Process: From BIOS to Kernel 44
  4.5. Securing the Kernel: Best Practices 47

5. Kernel Development Process 51
  5.1. Contribution Guidelines and Ethics 51
  5.2. Understanding Kernel Mailing Lists 54
  5.3. Version Control with Git 57
  5.4. Testing and Debugging Techniques 60
  5.5. Code Review and Mentoring New Developers 63

6. The Kernel Community and Ecosystem 68
  6.1. The Linux Foundation: Role and Influence 68
  6.2. Major Kernel Developers and Their Contributions 70
  6.3. Kernel Summits and Conferences 73
  6.4. Online Forums and Resources 76
  6.5. Collaborations and Partnerships 79

7. Performance Optimization 83
  7.1. Analyzing Your System's Performance 83
  7.2. Tuning the Kernel Parameters 85
  7.3. Tools for Monitoring and Profiling 88
  7.4. Best Practices for Optimization 91
  7.5. Common Pitfalls to Avoid 93

8. The Art of Kernel Hacking **97**

8.1. Kernel Hacking Essentials 97

8.2. Dealing with Kernel Panics and Crashes 99

8.3. Noise in Code: Cleaning Up Legacy Code 102

8.4. Creating Custom Kernel Modules 104

8.5. Security Concerns in Kernel Code 107

9. Real-time Kernel and Embedded Systems **111**

9.1. Understanding Real-time Expectations 111

9.2. Implementing Real-time Features 113

9.3. The Role of Linux in IoT 116

9.4. Challenges in Embedded Linux Systems 118

9.5. Case Studies of Real-time Applications 121

10. Open Source Philosophy and Ethics **125**

10.1. The Spirit of Open Source 125

10.2. Licensing and Legal Issues 127

10.3. Open Source Contributions and Etiquette 130

10.4. The Impact of Open Source on Society 132

10.5. Navigating Open Source Communities 135

11. Security and Privacy in Linux **139**

11.1. Kernel Security Features and Tools 139

11.2. Privacy Concerns in Kernel Development 142

11.3. Mitigating Security Vulnerabilities 144

11.4. Security-focused Kernel Distros 147

11.5. Developing for Secure Systems 150

"Open Source is the future of not just software but of business, as well."

— Matt Mullenweg

1. Introduction to the World of Linux Kernels

In the vast tapestry of modern computing, the Linux kernel emerges as an elusive and enigmatic entity that underpins much of what we take for granted in today's technological ecosystem. For many, it remains an unseen force, quietly humming in the background as they browse the internet, stream videos, or even launch spacecrafts. But what exactly is the Linux kernel, and why should it matter to you? nnIn this book, we will embark on an exploration of the heart of Linux, venturing into the realm where code and creativity intertwine. Whether you are a seasoned developer, a curious student, or simply someone fascinated by the pulse of technology, this journey promises to be enlightening. We will delve into the kernel's architecture, unravel its mysteries, and summon the spirits that have contributed to its evolution. nnSo, if you have ever knocked at the door of knowledge, yearning for a deeper understanding of how your devices tick, then you have indeed come to the right threshold. As we stand at the doorway of the kernel, poised to enter, remember: every grand innovation begins as a whispered idea in the mind of a dreamer. Welcome to "Knocking Kernel's Door: Summoning Linux's Kernel Spirits." May learning lead us into the profound depths of discovery and inspiration.

2. The Genesis of Linux

2.1. A Brief History of Operating Systems

To fully appreciate the significance and evolution of operating systems, it is essential to reflect on their historical journey, marked by innovative milestones and pivotal transformations that have shaped the computing experience we know today.

The earliest operating systems emerged in the 1950s, primarily designed for large mainframe computers. These systems were rudimentary, primarily focusing on batch processing where jobs were submitted to the computer to be processed sequentially. One of the inaugural operating systems was GM-NAA I/O, created for the IBM 704, which streamlined job management by automating input-output operations. This marked a significant shift from manual operation to programmatic control, setting the stage for future advancements.

As technology progressed through the 1960s, the demand for more interactive and efficient computing systems began to grow. This decade witnessed the emergence of multiprogramming and time-sharing systems, allowing multiple users to interact with the computer simultaneously. Operating systems like CTSS (Compatible Time-Sharing System) at MIT became pivotal by enabling users to run programs concurrently, enhancing the utility of mainframe machines. By creating a layered interface between the hardware and the user, these systems democratized access to computing resources.

The introduction of the Unix operating system in 1969 by Ken Thompson, Dennis Ritchie, and others at AT&T's Bell Labs represented a groundbreaking moment in operating system history. Unix adopted a modular design, offering portability, multitasking, and a multi-user environment. Its philosophy of using simple, interchangeable tools and a hierarchical file system inspired future operating systems, including Linux. The Unix time-sharing system encouraged networked computing, laying the groundwork for the distributed systems we see today.

As we entered the 1980s, personal computers began to proliferate, leading to the creation of new operating systems aimed at this burgeoning market. Microsoft's DOS (Disk Operating System) became the dominant OS for PCs, primarily due to its compatibility with IBM's personal computers. DOS's command-line interface was straightforward but eventually paved the way for more advanced graphical user interfaces (GUIs), such as those seen in Microsoft Windows, which gained immense popularity in the 1990s.

The period also saw a growing interest in open-source software, culminating in the establishment of the Free Software Foundation (FSF) in 1985. The FSF aimed to promote the creation and sharing of free software, which aligned with the principles set forth by Richard Stallman. This movement laid the groundwork for the collaborative development model that would flourish in the following decades.

The dawn of the 1990s marked the arrival of Linux, which began as a personal project by a Finnish student, Linus Torvalds. Inspired by the principles of Unix and driven by the ideals of collaboration and free software, Torvalds released the first version of the Linux kernel in 1991. What started as a small community project quickly evolved into a global phenomenon, as countless developers began contributing to its development, leading to an operating system that was robust, versatile, and community-driven.

The Linux kernel's evolution was marked by its adaptability and support for an extensive range of hardware, becoming a favorite among developers and server administrators alike. Its open-source nature allowed anyone to review, modify, and distribute the source code, fostering a vibrant ecosystem characterized by collaboration and shared knowledge.

The late 1990s and early 2000s further propelled Linux into the mainstream, driven by its burgeoning adoption in server environments, supercomputers, and eventually, the rise of the internet. Distributions like Red Hat, Debian, and later Ubuntu began to emerge, simplifying the installation and use of Linux for non-technical users. Businesses quickly recognized the cost-effectiveness and reliability of Linux, thus seizing opportunities to capitalize on its development.

As we navigated through the 21st century, operating systems diversified, reflecting different user needs and technological advancements. Modern operating systems now emphasize security, multitasking, and user experience, with Linux at the forefront. Its influence extends beyond traditional computing environments, as it has become integral in embedded systems, mobile devices (exemplified by Android), and cloud infrastructures.

The journey of operating systems has been one of continuous innovation, responding to the evolving requirements of users and advancements in hardware. Linux, as a representative of this evolution, embodies the spirit of collaboration, adaptability, and resilience. Understanding this history enriches our journey into the intricacies of the Linux kernel, revealing how it acts as both a product of its predecessors and a pioneer of new frontiers in technology.

2.2. The Birth of Linux: Ideals and Origins

In the grand narrative of technological advancement, the story of Linux is not just about code; it embodies a convergence of ideals, collaborative spirits, and the relentless pursuit of freedom in computing. The genesis of Linux owes much not only to technical aspirations but also to a philosophy that prioritizes openness, inclusivity, and communal effort.

At the heart of Linux's birth lies the influential and transformative movement of open-source software, deeply rooted in the lingering ideologies from early software development. The Free Software Foundation (FSF), established in the 1980s by Richard Stallman, was a pivotal catalyst in championing the concept of user freedom. Stallman's efforts were grounded in the belief that software should be free—not merely as a price point, but in the sense of freedom for users to study, modify, and distribute software. This ethos was crucial for what would eventually inspire Linus Torvalds in his own journey toward creating Linux.

Linus Torvalds, a Finnish computer science student, emerged onto the scene in 1991, driven by a desire to create a free alternative to the MINIX operating system, originally designed for educational purposes and navigating constraints imposed by proprietary systems. Despite the limited power and resources available to him, Torvalds' vision was shaped by a blend of necessity and ambition, propelled by a fundamental commitment to user freedom and collaborative development.

The pivotal moment arrived when Torvalds announced his project to the world on a now-famous Usenet post. His message read not just as a technical specification or a project outline, but as a call to arms, inviting collaboration: "I'm doing a (free) operating system (just a hobby, won't be big and professional like GNU)." This seemingly simple declaration resonated across the globe. It brought together a diverse group of developers, hobbyists, and intellectuals, all driven by a common pursuit—to craft a superior, open-source operating system that could thrive outside the rigid limitations of proprietary software.

The essence of Linux was thus born from a perfect alignment of technological need and idealistic vision. Its core principles echoed the purpose behind the FSF's foundation: empowering developers and users by dismantling the gates that typically constrain software access. This initial project was not just about creating a functional operating system; it represented a rebellion against the suffocating monopolies of the tech industry and an assertion of the values of cooperation and collective progress.

With its roots firmly planted in the Unix philosophy—embracing simplicity, modularity, and the utilization of small, composable tools —Linux was designed for efficiency and flexibility. Unlike its predecessors, which often charged hefty fees for licenses and support, Linux thrived on the collaborative spirit of its contributors. Code contributions poured in, and it was this communal effort that sparked rapid advancements and iterations of the kernel, with developers globally contributing their expertise and addressing varying issues faced by users.

As the Linux kernel evolved, it reflected the dynamic needs and voices of its community, with Torvalds serving not merely as a leader but as a custodian of the kernel's integrity and vision. His thoughtful governance allowed for diverse contributions while maintaining the system's coherence. Each new version was not just a technical update; it represented myriad hands and minds coalescing toward a shared goal.

The enthusiasm for Linux spread like wildfire, catalyzing movements that would enhance its reach and accessibility. Distributions emerged, each embodying unique philosophies and catering to different user demographics—ranging from programmers and system administrators to everyday users seeking alternatives to mainstream operating systems. These variations spotlighted Linux's modularity and adaptability while reinforcing its fundamental ethos of community and contribution.

The rise of Linux also coincided with the burgeoning internet era, where connectivity enabled developers to collaborate in real-time across the globe. This potentially allowed Linux to take root in server environments, data centers, and, later, mobile devices, marking its territory in domains where reliability and performance were paramount. As organizations recognized the value of an operating system that was not only comprehensive but also driven by a community ethos, they began adopting Linux, further cementing its relevance in the technology space.

In this ever-evolving landscape, the ideals and origins of Linux stand as a testament to the power of collective human endeavor. It is a narrative woven with terms of collaboration, resilience, and the unwavering belief that technology should not belong to a single entity but be accessible to all who wish to shape it. The birth of Linux transformed the horizons of software development and digital innovation, setting a precedent that inspired not just operating systems, but entire movements dedicated to software freedom and collaborative progress.

Thus, as we unravel the story of Linux, we learn that its simplest beginnings did not stem from a mere desire to create an operating system, but rather from a dream of liberation for all its users—an aspiration that breathes life into every line of code in the kernel's extensive tapestry. The legacy of Sigma's first steps into this world continues to resonate, encouraging future generations to keep knocking on the door of creativity, exploration, and emancipation that Linux so proudly stands for. Ultimately, the birth of Linux is anchored in ideals that reflect our highest aspirations for technology, fostering a culture rich in collaboration, freedom, and shared knowledge, each kernel spirit contributing to the greater good.

2.3. Linus Torvalds and the Iconic 'Hello World'

Linus Torvalds stands as an emblematic figure not just in the realm of technology but also in the broader narrative of open-source philosophy. His journey, from an inquisitive student at the University of Helsinki to the creator of one of the most widely used operating systems, encapsulates the spirit of innovation and collaboration. At the heart of this venture was a simple program, one that echoed through the annals of programming: the iconic "Hello World."

The origins of the "Hello World" program trace back to the early days of computer programming and is often regarded as the first application that novice programmers write when learning a new language. But its significance transcends mere functionality; it acts as an entry point into the world of coding, a symbolic initiation into the creativity and logic inherent to software development. For Linus Torvalds, his own "Hello World" marked the first steps into what would become a monumental project: the Linux kernel.

When Torvalds first conceptualized Linux in 1991, he was primarily motivated by a desire to create a free, Unix-like operating system. He embarked on this quest with a limited set of resources, but he was fueled by a firm belief in the open-source ideals nurtured by the Free Software Foundation led by Richard Stallman. The early iterations of the Linux kernel were forged from a modest vision, channeling the UNIX philosophy of simplicity and modular design. As he penned the initial lines of code, Torvalds infused them with dual aspirations: to learn and to share.

The moment he unveiled his work via a Usenet post was one of profound significance. With an almost casual command, he declared, "I'm doing a (free) operating system (just a hobby, won't be big and professional like GNU)." This succinct yet inviting announcement effectively served as his own "Hello World" to the global developer community. It beckoned those who shared his ambition, welcoming contributions from programmers everywhere. This eagerness to engage and share knowledge was not a mere afterthought; it was intrinsic to the project's direction from the outset.

As Linux garnered attention, Torvalds recognized that the simplest of concepts, like a "Hello World" program, could resonate deeply. It symbolized connectivity, curiosity, and the democratization of software. The act of running this basic program signified a user's command of the language and a connection to the underlying computer system. Torvalds' appeal for collaboration transformed his solitary endeavor into a collective movement, illustrating how even a humble beginning could resonate across borders and disciplines.

The power of "Hello World" lies in its ability to break barriers and foster community among budding developers. As participants began to contribute to the Linux kernel, they were not just engineering software; they were building a narrative—a shared space where ideas converged and flourished. Each contributor, much like those who write their own variations of "Hello World," introduced unique perspectives and expertise to the project. The kernel evolved, reflecting a mosaic of these diverse contributions, each piece adding depth and functionality.

Torvalds' role as both creator and curator was vital. He instituted a development style founded on meritocracy, encouraging contributions based on skill and creativity rather than hierarchy or position within companies. The open-source license allowed anyone to access, modify, and redistribute the code, facilitating widespread experimentation and innovation. The kernel's rapid advancement stands as testament to the collective ethos Torvalds nurtured—where even the smallest contributions mattered and every participant contributed to the strength of the project.

In many ways, the code of the Linux kernel embodies the spirit of "Hello World." It is resilient yet elegant, built on the foundational principles of simplicity and openness. As developers learned to navigate the complexities of the kernel, they often began with the same echoes of simplicity that characterized Torvalds' initial project. Their engagement served not only to broaden the kernel's capabilities, but to amplify the very ideals that it represented. The community that blossomed around Linux formed a successor to the principle of open and free software that Torvalds could have hardly imagined at the beginning of his journey.

As technological landscapes have transformed, so too has the interpretation and impact of "Hello World." It is now emblematic of the larger open-source movement—signifying not just the initiation of a programming journey, but the ethos of empowerment, collaboration, and relentless pursuit of improvement that permeates the Linux community. Moreover, as Linux continues to serve a multitude of applications, from servers to smartphones, the foundational message embedded in "Hello World" remains intact: the belief that software should be in the hands of all, crafted collectively for the greater good.

The evolution of the Linux kernel is thus intertwined with the narrative of its creator and the community that surrounds him. It's a story that encourages aspiring developers to take that curious leap into code, where each "Hello World" they write is a step into larger complexities and capabilities. Linus Torvalds, through his initial endeavor and subsequent stewardship, not only charged through the door of innovation but also opened it wide for countless others to follow. In this sense, "Hello World" transcends a simple output of text; it resonates as a clarion call for all who wish to innovate, discover, and forge new pathways in technology—a legacy forged in code that continuously inspires and invites anyone willing to contribute.

2.4. From Unix to Linux: The Transformation

In the realms of operating systems, the transition from Unix to Linux is not merely a chronological evolution but a profound transformation steeped in philosophy, community, and development practices. This metamorphosis reflects the shifting landscape of computing from closed, proprietary systems to open, collaborative environments. To unravel the complexities of this transformation, we must examine the historical context, technological innovations, and the cultural underpinnings that distinguished Unix from Linux.

Unix, developed in the late 1960s at AT&T's Bell Labs, established a solid foundation for operating systems with its modular architecture, multitasking capabilities, and multi-user environment. Its design philosophy emphasized simplicity and the use of small, composable utilities that perform specific tasks. These principles laid the groundwork for a suite of diverse and powerful tools that could be combined in myriad ways. Over the decades, Unix grew into a dominant operating system for servers and high-end workstations, spawning several variants, including AIX, HP-UX, and Solaris. However, its proprietary nature meant that the source code was tightly controlled, restricting access and collaborative development.

The arrival of Linux in 1991 signaled a turning point in this narrative. Linus Torvalds, inspired by Unix's architecture and motivated by the ideals of free software, initiated a project that fundamentally altered the expectations surrounding operating systems. Rather than adhering to the traditional routes of commercial software distribution, Linux epitomized open collaboration. Torvalds released the Linux kernel under the GNU General Public License (GPL), which enshrined user freedoms to run, modify, and distribute the software. This singular decision propelled Linux into a global movement, inviting contributions from experienced developers, hobbyists, and enthusiasts worldwide.

The technical innovations facilitated by this transformation are equally noteworthy. One of the hallmark features of Linux is its modular design. While Unix adhered to a monolithic kernel architecture, where the core functions were integrated, Linux's approach allows modules to be loaded and unloaded dynamically. This fosters flexibility, enabling users to tailor the system to their specific needs without necessitating a complete system overhaul. This adaptability boosts performance as well, as users can optimize their systems according to the workload demands - an attribute particularly crucial for diverse environments ranging from personal computers to industrial servers.

Moreover, the Linux transformation is punctuated by a reverence for community-driven development. With the advent of the internet, the barriers that once constrained collaboration began to dissolve. Developers from varied backgrounds could connect through mailing lists and forums, sharing patches, ideas, and expertise in real-time. Unlike Unix, which thrived within the parameters set by corporations, the Linux community embraced a meritocratic ethos, valuing contributions based on their effectiveness rather than the contributor's affiliation or stature. This dynamic not only promoted rapid development but also fostered a rich ecosystem of distributions, each with its own philosophy and purpose, catering to various user bases—from enterprise solutions to educational platforms.

Furthermore, the transformation from Unix to Linux also involved a shift in the narrative around user empowerment. In a Unix-controlled environment, users typically encountered a hierarchy of access and functionality, with tightly managed rights and controls. In contrast, Linux empowered users by giving them the keys to their computing experience. They could inspect the source code, modify it, and contribute to its development, fundamentally redefining the boundaries of user agency and autonomy. This cultural ethos attracted developers who sought not merely to use software but to understand and, when needed, reimagine it.

Another facet of this transformation lies in the comprehensive support for a plethora of hardware architectures that Linux adopted early on. While many Unix systems were confined to specialized hardware, Linux emerged as a versatile player, capable of running on anything from mainstream desktops to supercomputers. This adaptability accompanied by an open-source licensing model positioned Linux as a viable alternative across diverse technology stacks, ensuring its presence in embedded systems, consumer electronics, and the rapidly expanding clout of cloud technologies.

The evolution from Unix to Linux illustrates significant turning points not just in type and function but also in societal impact. Linux, as a manifestation of open source principles, sparked a revolution beyond its function as an operating system. It catalyzed a global movement advocating for transparency, cooperation, and innovation, impacting everything from academic research to corporate strategy. The ripple effects of Linux's success quashed myths about proprietary software dominance, empowering alternative operating systems to emerge and thrive, ensuring that the conversation around computing remains fluid, inclusive, and generally skewed towards collective development.

In conclusion, the transition from Unix to Linux represents a rich tapestry of technological evolution interwoven with principles of free and open software. This transformation reflects a paradigm shift, broadening access, empowering users, and fostering collaboration across borders and disciplines. As we delve deeper into the intricacies of the Linux kernel and its architecture, we must carry with us the understanding that the essence of Linux is not merely in its lines of code but in the spirit of community and innovation that continues to transcend traditional boundaries. The lore of Unix and Linux is not merely a tale of operating systems but a significant chapter in the ongoing journey towards collaborative technological growth and user empowerment in an ever-evolving digital landscape.

2.5. Early Challenges in Development

The path to the robust and versatile Linux kernel we know today was not paved without its share of challenges, particularly during its early stages of development. As Linus Torvalds initiated the project in 1991, he encountered a plethora of intricate issues that tested the resolve and ingenuity of not only himself but also the community that began to coalesce around him. Understanding these early challenges provides key insights into the kernel's eventual evolution and adaptability as a collaborative software project.

At the outset, the primary challenge for Torvalds lay in creating something functional on a very limited foundation. Having only a modest vision of producing a free operating system mimicking MINIX, he needed to overcome the constraints of limited resources and documentation. During this precipitating moment, significant hurdles included grappling with hardware limitations, inadequate underlying support, and the complexities of programming a multitasking kernel. Many early contributors possessed varying degrees of experience, leading to occasional inconsistencies in coding practices and understandings of design principles.

Hardware compatibility stood as one of the most challenging obstacles in the kernel's development. When Torvalds first envisioned Linux, personal computers were splintered into myriad systems with varying architecture. Ensuring that Linux could support different hardware—ranging from simple desktop peripherals to complex network interfaces—demanded exhaustive effort. As an integral component of the operating system, the kernel needed to interface with the spectrum of device drivers, each requiring tailored coding practices. This evolving landscape required Torvalds and early contributors to balance a sense of ambition with realistic limitations while engaging with the multitude of architectures that characterized the rapidly growing computing environment of the time.

Additionally, Torvalds faced resistance from the dominant narratives of the tech industry, which was, at the time, heavily skewed toward proprietary software models. The prevailing wisdom dictated that quality software required commercial backing and corporate resources. Convincing developers and users to embrace the idea that a community-driven, open-source alternative could attain the levels of robustness and security they sought proved daunting. Cultivating trust among prospective contributors and users required careful navigation of skepticism while establishing a framework for governance that encouraged inclusivity and responsibility.

As contributions began to pour in, the community faced challenges intrinsic to collaboration. Unlike singularly owned projects, the Linux kernel development required developers from various backgrounds and expertise to work in harmony, with differing views on the direction of the kernel often leading to conflicts. Building a cohesive direction demanded careful stewardship from Torvalds, who took on the weighty task of fostering an environment conducive to innovation while mediating disputes and expectations among contributors. By establishing guidelines and a clear versioning strategy, he helped mitigate redundancies and managed potential fragmentation among code contributions.

The collaborative nature of Linux development presented another potential pitfall. With the rise of a distributed developer community, tracking contributions and ensuring the integrity of the kernel's codebase became increasingly complex. The task of patch management required rigorous practices to evaluate code submissions, ensuring that they met quality standards and aligned with the overarching goals of the project. This quality control became increasingly vital as the kernel matured, prompting Torvalds to put forth calls for more transparency and systematic processes for reviewing changes —a practice that would later evolve into formalized development protocols.

Security, too, posed an existential challenge during the kernel's early evolution. As an open-source project, Linux initially did not have the comprehensive security frameworks that would later evolve. Vulnerabilities in the codebase could potentially compromise not just the kernel but user data and system integrity as well. Consequently, early iterations involved a learning journey regarding principles of secure coding, with contributors needing to study exploits and mitigate risks continuously. Torvalds and the community realized that fostering a culture of vigilance toward security was essential to nurturing both the project's longevity and the trust of its user base.

A pivotal turning point came with the emergence of the internet, which facilitated communication and collaboration at an unprecedented scale. New mailing lists and forums where users and developers could discuss issues, showcase breakthroughs, and share solutions became instrumental in overcoming early hurdles. Each interaction allowed the community to rise from trial to success, creating a roadmap toward collective problem-solving and a shared sense of accomplishment.

As various contributors began to amass expertise in addressing the substantial challenges of developing an operating system, the success of the early efforts planted the seeds for a thriving ecosystem. The experiences gathered during these formative stages not only enhanced individual contributors' coding skills but also fostered a deep appreciation for the collaborative spirit that Linux came to embody. Through trial and error, successes and setbacks, the community learned important lessons about handling disagreements, aligning goals, and appreciating the contributions of every participant, major or minor.

In retrospect, the early challenges faced in the Linux kernel's development served not only to test the resolve of its instigators but also to shape the principles and practices that continue to guide its evolution. Each obstacle reinforced the importance of open communication, collaborative problem-solving, and a commitment to shared ideals in addressing the complexities of software development. As Linux emerged from its nascent phases into a robust, enterprise-grade operating system, it lay a foundation built upon resilience, adaptability, and the unwavering belief in technology as a collective endeavor— not simply a tool, but a shared journey into the future of computing. The kernel that continues to power countless systems today stands as a testament to the triumphs and trials of those early days, embodying a spirit of collaboration that has reverberated throughout technology history.

3. Understanding the Linux Kernel

3.1. What is a Kernel?

In the study of computer science and software engineering, the term "kernel" holds profound significance as it represents a fundamental component of an operating system. The kernel serves as a bridge between the hardware and the software applications that run on a system, managing resources, enabling communication, and providing essential services. Within the context of Linux, the kernel is not merely a piece of software; it embodies the very spirit of the operating system, reflecting its ideals of openness and collaboration.

At its core, a kernel is responsible for managing the system's resources, including the CPU, memory, and input/output devices. It efficiently allocates these resources among various processes, ensuring that they can operate concurrently without conflict. This resource management encompasses several critical roles: process scheduling, memory management, device management, and system calls.

Process scheduling is the mechanism through which the kernel decides which processes receive CPU time and for how long. Given the multi-tasking capabilities of modern operating systems, the kernel must juggle numerous processes, each with differing priorities. The kernel employs various scheduling algorithms to optimize CPU usage and responsiveness, ranging from simple round-robin strategies to more complex priority-based systems. By effectively managing process scheduling, the kernel ensures that users can run multiple applications simultaneously without significant performance degradation.

Memory management is another pivotal function of the kernel, which oversees how memory is allocated and accessed by different processes. The kernel maintains a memory map, tracking which portions of memory are in use and which are free. It employs techniques such as paging and segmentation to efficiently utilize memory resources, allowing for greater flexibility and security. Paging, for example, divides memory into fixed-size blocks, enabling the kernel to load only the necessary parts of a program into memory, thereby optimizing performance and minimizing resource wastage.

Device management involves the kernel acting as an intermediary between system hardware and software. The kernel interacts with various hardware components through device drivers, which are specialized pieces of code that translate the general commands issued by software applications into hardware-specific instructions. This abstraction allows software developers to write applications without needing deep knowledge of the underlying hardware, simplifying the development process and enhancing portability across different hardware configurations.

In the Linux kernel, system calls serve as the primary interface between user-space applications and the kernel itself. When a program requires a service from the operating system—such as reading from a file or creating a new process—it makes a system call. The kernel processes these calls, performs the necessary operations, and returns the results to the requesting application. This interaction forms the backbone of application functionality, demonstrating the kernel's integral role in facilitating user interactions with the system.

The design of the Linux kernel is characterized by several key attributes that elevate its functionality and adaptability. One of the most prominent features is its monolithic architecture, which integrates numerous services into a single address space. This contrasts with microkernel architectures, where the kernel operates with minimal services, delegating additional functionalities to user-space servers. The monolithic design enables faster communication between components but also raises concerns about stability and security; a bug in the kernel can lead to system-wide failures. On the other hand, the Linux kernel's extensive testing and robust community practices mitigate many of these risks.

Another important aspect of the Linux kernel is its modularity. While the kernel operates as a monolithic system, it supports dynamic loading of modules. Modules are pieces of code that can be loaded and unloaded at runtime, allowing the kernel to extend its capabilities without requiring a complete reboot. This modularity enhances the kernel's flexibility, enabling it to adapt to a wide variety of hardware and user requirements. Developers can create custom modules for specific functionalities, such as file systems or networking protocols, offering users tailored solutions without compromising the integrity of the overall system.

Moreover, the evolution of the Linux kernel has been heavily influenced by the principles of open source. The kernel's source code is freely available to the public, allowing anyone to inspect, modify, or contribute to its development. This open-source paradigm encourages collaboration and rapid innovation, as developers worldwide can collaborate on improvements and share their findings. The Linux community embodies a culture of knowledge-sharing, fostering an environment where contributors learn from one another and collectively enhance the kernel's quality and functionality.

Over the years, the development of the Linux kernel has seen its fair share of challenges and triumphs. From early struggles with hardware compatibility to the complexities of managing contributions from a global community, the kernel's journey reflects the dynamic nature of collaborative software development. The early phases were marked by experimentation, as developers navigated the intricacies of both the code and the principles of open source. With each iteration, the Linux kernel evolved, addressing shortcomings, enhancing performance, and expanding compatibility, all driven by a dedicated and passionate community.

In conclusion, the Linux kernel is the lifeblood of the Linux operating system—an intricate, multifaceted component that plays an essential role in resource management, application support, and hardware integration. The kernel's evolution, grounded in principles of openness and collaboration, showcases how communities can harness the collective power of innovation and creativity to produce software that is robust, versatile, and adaptable. As we delve deeper into the specifics of Linux kernel architecture, key components, interfaces, and subsystems, we embark on a journey to understand not just the mechanics of technology, but the rich tapestry of human endeavor woven into every line of code.

3.2. Key Components: From Scheduler to Memory Management

The Linux kernel is a complex and multifaceted structure composed of various critical components that work in concert to manage and optimize system resources. Understanding this architecture provides valuable insight into how the kernel operates and how it supports numerous applications across a myriad of environments.

One of the indispensable components of the kernel is the scheduler. The scheduler is the core mechanism responsible for managing CPU time among various processes running simultaneously. It is designed to ensure fairness and efficiency in resource allocation, allowing multiple applications to coexist without significant performance degradation. In essence, the scheduler is tasked with deciding which process gets to run at any given moment. There are several scheduling algorithms implemented in the Linux kernel, each catering to different needs and scenarios. The Completely Fair Scheduler (CFS) is the default in modern Linux distributions, designed to provide fair allocation of CPU time by tracking how much time each process has used and ensuring that they all receive their fair share over time. Other algorithms, such as the Real-Time Scheduler, prioritize time-sensitive processes, making them ideal for applications where responsiveness is critical, such as audio processing or industrial automation.

Following closely behind scheduling, memory management is another critical component of the Linux kernel. At its most basic level, memory management entails the allocation and deallocation of memory space as processes require it, while efficiently utilizing the available memory. The kernel tracks which portions of memory are currently in use or available through a complex data structure called the memory map. Virtual memory, an essential feature of Linux, allows the system to use disk space to simulate additional RAM.

This enables larger applications to run even when physical memory resources are limited. Moreover, the kernel implements various mechanisms like paging and swapping to optimize memory use and ensure that active processes do not interfere with one another via memory isolation.

Device management forms another essential piece of the kernel's architecture. The kernel directly interacts with hardware through device drivers: specialized modules within the kernel that facilitate communication between the operating system and the hardware peripherals. Each piece of hardware—be it a hard disk, network card, or graphics processor—requires a specific driver to enable proper functionality. The kernel abstracts hardware complexities, allowing application developers to interact with devices uniformly, without needing to know the details of the underlying hardware. This abstraction not only streamlines the development process but also enhances portability as applications can run across different hardware platforms with minimal adjustments.

In addition to these components, system calls serve as the connective tissue that allows user-space applications to interact with the kernel and leverage its functionalities. When a program needs to execute an operation that requires access to hardware or requires other system resources, it invokes a system call that transitions control from user space to kernel space. The kernel processes the request and returns the appropriate results to the user-space application. This interaction is central to the typical flow of operations in a Linux system, making system calls crucial for effective resource management.

The architectural choices within the Linux kernel contribute significantly to its versatility and capability across numerous use cases. One of the defining features of the kernel's design is its monolithic architecture. Unlike microkernels that attempt to run most services in user space and maintain only the essential components within the kernel, the monolithic architecture incorporates a wide array of services within the main kernel space. While this can lead to increased risks of instability—since any fault in the kernel can crash the entire system—it also facilitates high performance due to reduced context switching and faster communication between components.

Despite its monolithic structure, the Linux kernel embraces modularity, allowing additional functionalities to be loaded as needed via dynamically loadable kernel modules (LKMs). This flexibility enables users to customize and optimize their kernel configurations without needing a complete recompilation. System administrators can add or remove features as their requirements evolve, such as supporting new hardware or enabling specific protocols, all without rebooting the system. This level of adaptability marks a significant advantage for Linux, particularly in environments with varying workloads and hardware configurations.

A significant influence on the development and functionality of the Linux kernel emerges from the ethos of open-source collaboration. The kernel's source code is available for public review and modification, fostering an active community of developers who contribute to its ongoing evolution. This spirit of collaboration has led to a continuously improving codebase, enriched by diverse contributions and extensive testing from users across the globe.

To comprehend the complete picture, it's essential to recognize the Linux kernel not as an isolated entity but as an integral part of a broader operating system ecosystem. The kernel interfaces with user-space applications, manages resources, communicates with hardware, and provides essential services to ensure a coherent computing experience. Understanding these key components—ranging from the scheduler to memory management, device communication, and user interactions through system calls—reveals the intricate workings of the Linux kernel and the dynamic interplay that allows it to serve a wide range of applications across diverse computing environments effectively.

As we continue to explore the architecture of the Linux kernel, we will delve deeper into kernel interfaces, subsystems, and the contrasts between user space and kernel space, laying the groundwork for a comprehensive understanding of the diverse functionalities that comprise this powerful and versatile operating system. Each component, each interaction and each design choice ultimately reflects the collaborative spirit that defines Linux's legacy, continually driving the evolution of technology in a shared pursuit of innovation and accessibility.

3.3. Kernel Interfaces and APIs

Kernel interfaces and APIs are essential facets of the Linux kernel that facilitate interaction between software applications and the underlying hardware. The design principles governing these interfaces and application programming interfaces (APIs) not only streamline the development process but also enhance system performance and maintainability. A thorough understanding of these elements is vital for any developer looking to harness the full potential of the Linux kernel.

At its core, the kernel interface serves as a communication bridge between user-space applications and kernel space. It abstracts low-level hardware details and provides a set of standardized operations that applications can invoke to interact with the system. This abstraction is crucial as it enables developers to write high-level code without delving into the complexities of hardware communication. The kernel provides a well-defined interface for performing various actions, such as managing processes, accessing files, and interacting with network interfaces.

System calls constitute the primary mechanism through which user-space applications access the kernel's services. When a process needs to request a specific service, such as reading data from disk or allocating memory, it issues a system call. The invocation formats the request, which the CPU processes in user mode. The transition from user space to kernel space is crucial, as it ensures that the kernel maintains control over system resources and enforces security measures. The kernel processes the request, executes the required action, and passes back any results to the calling process before returning to user space.

Linux defines a rich set of system calls, which are organized into groups based on functionality. For example, file system operations are handled through a specific set of system calls that allow applications to open, read, write, and close files. Similarly, process control functions allow applications to create, terminate, and manage processes. This organization not only enhances usability but also simplifies the implementation of new kernel features. Developers can introduce additional system calls without disrupting existing APIs, facilitating backward compatibility for user applications.

The Kernel's Application Binary Interface (ABI) is another critical aspect of kernel interfaces, defining the low-level details associated with how programs interact. The ABI dictates specifics such as data types, structures, and calling conventions. Consistency in the ABI is paramount, as it allows applications to function consistently across different kernel versions. The stability of the ABI is particularly crucial for commercial software and long-standing applications that may require continued compatibility with newer kernel versions.

Device drivers represent a vital interface between the kernel and hardware devices. They allow the kernel to communicate with various hardware components, such as disk drives, printers, and network interfaces. Device drivers operate under the kernel's standard interface mechanisms, allowing applications to interact with hardware devices using a unified set of commands. Each device driver is designed to translate application-level requests into hardware-specific commands, managing the intricacies of device operation while ensuring seamless communication between hardware and kernel space.

In terms of data exchange, the Linux kernel employs various data structures, including queues and buffers. These components play a significant role in managing the flow of data between user-space applications and devices, facilitating efficient communication. For example, ring buffers are often used to manage input and output streams between devices and the kernel, ensuring smooth and efficient data transfer. The well-defined interfaces surrounding these data structures enable effective resource management and bolster overall system performance.

The kernel also provides facilities for inter-process communication (IPC), enabling processes to communicate with one another reliably. IPC mechanisms in Linux include pipes, message queues, shared memory, and semaphores. Each of these methods serves a specific purpose in enabling synchronization and communication between processes. For instance, pipes provide a unidirectional flow of data between processes, while message queues allow for asynchronous communication. These mechanisms enhance the multiprocessing capabilities of Linux, allowing developers to build complex applications that require coordination among multiple processes.

Another noteworthy aspect of kernel interfaces and APIs is their role in ensuring security and isolation within the system. The Linux kernel enforces strict permissions and access controls, determining which processes can access specific resources. The kernel employs user and group IDs to manage access rights, which play a crucial role in protecting sensitive information and system stability. Furthermore, the use of namespaces and control groups (cgroups) allows the creation of isolated environments, enabling container technologies to flourish within the Linux ecosystem. This isolation improves security by minimizing the potential attack surface while maximizing operational flexibility.

Additionally, the way in which threading is handled in Linux, through the implementation of the 'clone' system call, provides a modular interface. Threads in Linux are treated as lightweight processes that share resources, and they can be created swiftly without the overhead of full process creations. This approach enhances performance for applications requiring concurrent execution, laying the groundwork for multi-threaded programming in user space while leveraging the kernel's efficient resource management.

In a broader perspective, kernel interfaces and APIs have inherently aided the growth of a vibrant ecosystem of tools, libraries, and development environments that leverage the capabilities of the Linux kernel. As open-source software continues to thrive, contributions from developers globally enrich the API landscape, allowing developers to craft innovative applications and services that make optimal use of kernel functionalities. The evolution of interfaces within Linux not only reflects the advancements in technology but also showcases the collaborative spirit rooted in the principles of open-source development.

In conclusion, kernel interfaces and APIs form the backbone of the Linux operating system, enabling seamless communication between applications and the underlying hardware. By abstracting complexities, enforcing security measures, and providing a rich set of operations, the Linux kernel facilitates efficient resource management and robust application development. The design principles guiding kernel interfaces underscore the importance of usability, stability, and flexibility, allowing developers to harness the full spectrum of Linux capabilities. As we navigate through the dynamic landscape of Linux kernel evolution, understanding these elements provides clarity on the remarkable synergy between hardware and software that defines modern computing experiences.

3.4. Subsystems and Modules Explained

In the rich and intricate landscape of the Linux kernel, subsystems and modules serve as foundational elements that enable the operating system to function effectively across diverse computing environments. Understanding these components is crucial to grasping how the kernel manages resources, interacts with hardware, and supports the multitude of applications that run on Linux.

Subsystems are dedicated areas of the kernel that handle specific functionalities, allowing for organized and modular management of different system tasks. There are numerous subsystems within the Linux kernel, each serving a dedicated purpose that contributes to the overall efficiency, performance, and adaptability of the operating system. Some of the most notable subsystems include the process management subsystem, memory management subsystem, file system subsystem, device management subsystem, and networking subsystem, among others.

The process management subsystem is primarily responsible for managing the life cycle of processes within the system. It oversees the creation, scheduling, and termination of processes, ensuring that the CPU time is allocated efficiently across multiple tasks. This subsystem utilizes various scheduling algorithms to determine which processes should run at any given time, considering factors such as process priority and resource requirements. By effectively managing processes, the kernel ensures that applications run smoothly without conflicting for resources.

The memory management subsystem plays a critical role in the kernel's ability to handle tasks efficiently. This subsystem oversees the allocation and deallocation of memory, enabling processes to utilize system resources effectively. Memory management includes the implementation of techniques such as paging, segmentation, and virtual memory. By providing processes with the virtual address spaces they need while keeping physical memory usage optimized, the kernel enhances overall system performance.

In addition to process and memory management, the file system subsystem serves as an organized framework for data storage and retrieval. It provides the necessary APIs and tools for applications to interact with files, enabling actions such as creating, reading, updating, and deleting files. The kernel supports various file systems, such as ext4, XFS, and Btrfs, each impressing unique functionalities and performance characteristics that cater to different use cases.

Device management is another pivotal subsystem, functioning as the intermediary between hardware devices and the kernel itself. Device drivers, which reside within this subsystem, translate general commands issued by applications into specific instructions understood by different hardware components. The kernel abstracts the details of hardware interaction, allowing users and application developers to focus on higher-level functionality without needing in-depth knowledge of the underlying hardware.

The networking subsystem facilitates communication over networks, managing packet transmission, routing, and various protocols to ensure seamless data transfer between machines. This subsystem includes support for TCP/IP, UDP, and a variety of other networking protocols, reflecting the critical role that networking plays in modern computing.

Modules within the Linux kernel play a complementary role to subsystems. While subsystems represent specific functionalities, modules embody the dynamic extensibility of the kernel itself. Kernel modules are pieces of code that can be loaded and unloaded at runtime, allowing the kernel to adapt to varying system requirements without necessitating a full system reboot. This modularity is particularly advantageous in environments where hardware configurations may change frequently, or when specific functionalities need to be added or removed based on user preferences.

Each kernel module can represent a driver, a file system, or even an entirely new subsystem. By utilizing modules, administrators and developers can customize their kernel environments, loading only those features essential to their operations. This not only reduces the footprint of the operating system but also minimizes potential security vulnerabilities associated with unnecessary components.

The successful integration of subsystems and modules relies heavily on the cohesive nature of the Linux kernel's design—where these elements work together harmoniously. This design philosophy reflects the principles of openness and collaboration that are intrinsic to the Linux community. The open-source nature of the kernel means that anyone can inspect, modify, or contribute to its code, which fosters innovation, dissemination of knowledge, and rapid development cycles. As contributors from around the world develop modules or enhancements to existing subsystems, they engage in a cycle of continuous improvement, ultimately leading to a more robust and versatile operating system.

The accessibility and adaptability of subsystems and modules also promote a culture of experimentation and learning. Developers can test new ideas and functionalities without the constraints imposed by traditional, monolithic architectures. This environment encourages a diverse range of contributions that can lead to unexpected advancements and optimizations.

While subsystems and kernel modules contribute significantly to the kernel's capabilities, they also present their challenges. The integration of new modules or updates can introduce complexities that need to be carefully managed to avoid conflicts or regressions in system stability. The collaborative nature of the Linux community plays a pivotal role in addressing these challenges, as developers share experiences, best practices, and solutions to common issues.

Kernel development is further strengthened by comprehensive documentation and community resources that exist to guide contributors and users alike. Through documentation, forums, and mailing lists, developers can troubleshoot issues, seek guidance, and share their innovations, thus bolstering the ongoing evolution of the Linux kernel.

In summary, the interplay between subsystems and modules within the Linux kernel encapsulates the essence of effective resource management and adaptability in modern operating systems. As these components work in concert, they empower the Linux kernel to meet the demands of an ever-evolving technological landscape, offering the flexibility required to support a wide range of applications from servers to embedded systems and everything in between. Embracing the principles of collaboration and innovation, Linux stands as a testament to the dynamic nature of software development, where every contribution—whether a subsystem enhancement or a new module— helps build a stronger, more resilient architecture that resonates with the ideals of the open-source community. Through continual engagement and contribution, developers keep unlocking the potential of Linux, ensuring its relevance and vitality in the world of technology.

3.5. User Space vs. Kernel Space

The Linux operating system is fundamentally designed through two distinct realms known as user space and kernel space, each serving a crucial role in the interaction between software applications and hardware. Understanding the fundamental differences between these two spaces is vital for grasping how Linux operates and how the kernel manages crucial resources.

At the heart of this separation is the Linux kernel itself. Acting as a bridge between software and hardware, the kernel operates in kernel space, a protected area of memory reserved for the core functions of the operating system. In this realm, the kernel has unrestricted access to all system resources, including hardware components, memory, and processor capabilities. It performs essential functions such as process scheduling, memory management, and device management, ensuring that user applications can execute efficiently, securely, and without direct interference with hardware.

Kernel space is characterized by a higher level of privilege and control. When the kernel executes, it runs in what is referred to as "kernel mode," enabling it to perform sensitive operations that user space applications are not permitted to execute. This includes direct hardware access and the ability to manage interrupts, which are signals that inform the processor of events that need immediate attention. Because of this heightened authority, kernel mode is also riskier; a bug or error in the kernel can lead to system crashes or even catastrophic failures.

In contrast, user space is the avenue where user applications and processes reside, executing under a significantly different set of privileges. This separation is a deliberate design feature that enhances the stability and security of the operating system. Programs running in user space operate in "user mode," meaning they have limited access to system resources. They cannot directly interact with hardware or the memory space of other processes, which helps prevent malicious activities and the accidental destabilization of the operating system.

When a user-space application needs to perform an operation that requires kernel intervention, it must issue a system call. This serves as a controlled method for transitioning from user mode to kernel mode. Upon receiving a request, the kernel validates the request and then performs the specified operations on behalf of the process, returning the results back to user space. This mechanism not only maintains security but also controls how resources are shared among users and applications.

The distinction between user space and kernel space leads to considerable implications for system performance and stability. By enforcing strict boundaries, the Linux operating system minimizes the risk of bugs or errors in user applications affecting the core system. If a user-space application crashes, the kernel remains intact, and other programs continue to operate normally. However, if there is a flaw within the kernel itself, it can lead to a complete system failure.

This careful separation also presents certain challenges. While the kernel can manage resources effectively, the need to switch context between user space and kernel space can introduce latency. Each transition requires the CPU to switch modes, manipulating the stack, and saving and restoring contexts, which adds overhead. To mitigate performance impacts, Linux strives to minimize these transitions, optimizing how user-space applications interact with kernel functions.

Hardware drivers, crucial for facilitating communication between the kernel and hardware devices, primarily reside in kernel space. They manage the intricate details of device interaction while allowing user-space applications to access hardware features through well-defined APIs. This modular approach simplifies the complexity and allows developers to work with hardware without needing to delve into the underlying kernel code.

Security considerations further emphasize the importance of the user space and kernel space distinction. The kernel implements various access controls and permissions to manage resource allocation. When user-space applications request specific resources, the kernel enforces policies based on user rights and system configurations, ensuring that no single application can monopolize the system or disrupt the operations of others.

Additionally, the isolation provided by this separation fosters a safer environment for development. For instance, when developers create new software, they can do so without fear of crashing the entire system, as any faults will only impact their application. This encourages innovation and experimentation, allowing developers to push boundaries without exposing themselves or others to risk.

Another crucial aspect of this framework is the memory management model employed by the Linux kernel. Memory is organized in such a way that user processes are allocated their own virtual address space, which is isolated from the kernel's address space. This design prevents user processes from damaging or corrupting the kernel or other processes. Furthermore, the kernel takes responsibility for managing physical memory, deciding how much memory to allocate to user applications, thus maintaining system stability and performance despite varying workloads.

In summary, the distinction between user space and kernel space is a cornerstone of Linux's architecture, underscoring the necessity for security, efficiency, and stability in modern operating systems. By maintaining separate environments for user-level applications and kernel-level operations, Linux ensures that hardware resource management remains efficient while minimizing risks associated with application faults. This separation embodies the balance needed for fostering robust computing environments, allowing both users and developers to benefit from the advantages offered by one of the most powerful operating systems in existence. Ultimately, understanding user space vs. kernel space equips anyone delving into Linux with the foundational knowledge necessary to leverage the operating system effectively, paving the way for deeper exploration of its architecture and capabilities.

4. Linux Kernel Architecture

4.1. Monolithic vs. Microkernel Debate

The debate between monolithic kernels and microkernels is one of the fundamental discussions in operating system design, particularly within the context of Linux and its architectural philosophy. This sub-chapter aims to dissect the characteristics, benefits, and drawbacks of each approach, ultimately addressing how they influence not only the performance and efficiency of the kernel but also the dynamics of development and community involvement.

To initiate the discourse, we must first define the two architectures. A monolithic kernel, as implemented in Linux, is a single large program that includes all the essential operating system services, such as process management, memory management, device drivers, and file system management, operating in a single address space. In this model, system calls and other interactions between processes and the kernel happen directly within this address space, allowing for high-speed communication and efficient resource management. The Linux kernel exemplifies this design through its ability to dynamically load and unload modules as needed, thereby expanding its capabilities while retaining the core benefits of a monolithic structure.

Conversely, a microkernel architecture minimizes the functionalities embedded within the kernel itself, delegating most services to user-space servers. Essential kernel functions like memory management and task scheduling remain within the kernel space, but many drivers and additional services operate in user space. This architectural choice allows for greater modularity and enhances system stability, as errors in user-space services do not compromise the kernel's integrity. The microkernel, therefore, aspires for simplicity and relia-bility, promoting the idea that a minimal core can result in a more manageable and maintainable system.

One of the primary advantages of a monolithic kernel is performance. By residing within a single address space and executing most tasks with minimal context switching, monolithic systems tend to exhibit lower latency and higher throughput. For instance, operations such as inter-process communication are faster because they do not require the overhead associated with transitioning between user space and kernel space. This efficiency has been crucial for Linux, enabling it to perform exceptionally well across diverse workloads, from workstations to servers and embedded systems.

In contrast, while microkernels can often yield better reliability and security due to modular design, that comes at the cost of performance. The need for user-space servers to handle various tasks means that more context switches occur, which can introduce latency and complexity. Each request that traverses the user/kernel boundary involves significant overhead; while modern microkernel designs aim to mitigate these issues, performance remains a noted challenge compared to monolithic systems.

An additional point of contrast lies in the area of development and maintainability. The monolithic kernel's tightly integrated approach often results in more significant codebases, becoming harder for developers to navigate over time. This complexity can occasionally lead to bugs that impact the entire system. However, the Linux community has developed extensive testing frameworks and revision systems to counteract these challenges. The growth of a rich ecosystem around kernel development has also encouraged robust community practices, ensuring that contributions follow stringent quality guidelines.

On the other hand, the microkernel's modular nature fosters a more straightforward debugging process. Isolated components allow developers to address faults without the risk of compromising the entire system. This modularity coupled with clear API definitions can encourage collaboration as different teams focus on specific user-space functions without needing deep insights into the kernel code. However, ensuring that modules interact seamlessly remains a critical challenge, as coordination and communication between these services can become complicated.

Security emerges as another crucial point in this debate. Microkernels have a theoretical advantage thanks to their reduced attack surface; if most services run in user space, the kernel's core functions can remain shielded from potential vulnerabilities that arise from unstable or malicious drivers. This division minimizes the risk posed by a compromised component, as attackers would need to target individual user-space services to impact overall system functionality. Conversely, the monolithic kernel is indeed more exposed to potential security flaws given its expansive nature and complex integrations; however, the active and global Linux community ensures that updates are consistently rolled out to address vulnerabilities swiftly.

Furthermore, the choice of kernel architecture has a significant impact on the user and developer experience. Users of systems based on microkernels may benefit from configurations tailored for specific applications and environments, though they may face challenges with driver availability and integration. Conversely, the rich ecosystems developing around monolithic kernels like Linux have catalyzed extensive driver support and widespread adoption across devices, providing users with the power and flexibility needed to operate in a modern computing environment.

Historical choices have also played a role in shaping the current landscape of kernel debates. Initially, microkernels gained traction in academic environments, fostering interest in the potential benefits of modularity and simplicity. However, as practical implementation illuminated the performance issues those architectures faced, monolithic kernels gained favor in most commercial settings. The rise of Linux, with its monolithic yet modular architecture, reflects a middle ground that seeks to leverage the benefits of both paradigms.

In conclusion, the monolithic versus microkernel debate continues to be rich terrain for exploration and discussion. Monolithic kernels like Linux provide unmatched performance and expansive driver support, thanks to their tightly integrated architecture. In contrast, microkernels emphasize reliability and modularity, offering a more manageable approach. However, performance trade-offs often accompany this choice. The challenge lies in balancing the ideals of efficiency, maintainability, and security while fostering a vibrant community for collaboration and innovation. As technology evolves, so too will the discussions surrounding these kernel architectures, pushing boundaries and inviting new considerations about how we design and interact with our computing environments. In the realm of Linux development, this debate continues to ignite discussions, shaping not just the kernel's future but the trajectory of the entire open-source ecosystem.

4.2. The Modular Nature of Linux

The Linux kernel exemplifies a modular architecture that underpins its flexibility, extensibility, and resilience in various computing environments. This modular nature is essential for understanding how the kernel operates, adapts to hardware changes, and evolves through community-driven contributions. It embodies an essential framework that enhances resource management, allows for the dynamic addition of functionality, and supports a wide variety of applications.

At its core, the modular nature of Linux means that its design allows for different components—such as device drivers, file system support, and additional functionalities—to be developed and loaded independently. This modular approach facilitates numerous advantages that significantly enhance the operating system's performance, maintainability, and usability.

One of the most significant benefits of a modular kernel is the ability to load and unload modules dynamically at runtime. Unlike traditional monolithic kernels, which require a full recompilation and reboot to modify kernel functionalities, Linux modules can be added or removed as necessary. This process is usually accomplished through commands like `modprobe` and `rmmod`, which manage kernel modules and allow system administrators to extend or customize the kernel functionality without disrupting services.

Modularity is particularly advantageous in environments with diverse hardware configurations or specialized applications. For instance, in server environments, where resources may fluctuate based on workload demands, system administrators can tailor the kernel by loading specific modules that correspond to the required functionalities, thereby optimizing system performance without unnecessary overhead. Additionally, developers can create custom modules to support unique hardware devices, ensuring that the kernel remains adaptable to changing technological landscapes.

Moreover, the modular nature of Linux encourages a clean separation of responsibilities within the kernel architecture. Each module is typically responsible for a specific function, such as handling a particular file system type or managing a network interface. This separation not only aids developers in understanding and managing the kernel's structure but also enhances collaboration among contributors. Each developer can focus on writing and optimizing specific modules without needing to delve into the kernel's entirety, promoting efficiency and shared ownership of the codebase.

Beyond facilitating dynamic loading, the modularity of Linux also enhances security and stability. Bugs or errors experienced in one module do not compromise the entire kernel; instead, they can be isolated, allowing the system to maintain functionality through the remaining modules. In the event of a malfunctioning module, it can be unloaded or replaced without requiring a reboot, minimizing downtime and enhancing overall system resilience. This capability is particularly valuable in mission-critical environments where uptime is paramount.

The active participation of the open-source community has also enriched the modular aspect of the Linux kernel. With a vast array of contributors from different backgrounds, the community continuously develops and refines kernel modules. Each new version of the kernel incorporates improvements and additional module support, showcasing the collaborative spirit that underpins Linux's success. The development of modules often follows well-defined guidelines and protocols, enabling contributions that adhere to quality standards and maintain consistency across the kernel.

While the benefits of modularity are numerous, they do come with their inherent complexities. The interplay and dependencies between modules can create challenges, as modules that rely on one another must be managed carefully to ensure compatibility. The Linux kernel employs semantic versioning and other development practices to facilitate smooth integration and avoid conflicts that may arise from updates or changes in dependent modules.

The concept of modularity in Linux extends to the kernel's architecture, allowing for significant customization of various Linux distributions. Distributions can choose to enable or disable specific modules based on their target audience or application demands. For instance, systems designed for general-purpose use might incorporate a broad set of modules, while specialized embedded or real-time systems may load only the bare essentials. This adaptability ensures that Linux can thrive in a myriad of environments, from cloud servers to Internet of Things (IoT) devices.

Another interesting aspect of the modular nature of Linux is its emphasis on compatibility with legacy systems. As technologies evolve, some modules may become outdated or deprecated, yet the kernel can often still support these legacy modules. This capability ensures that organizations using older hardware or software can continue to operate seamlessly, minimizing disruption in environments where upgrading or replacing systems is unfeasible.

The process of developing and maintaining kernel modules is well-supported by a variety of tools and documentation provided by the Linux community. Developers can leverage build systems like kbuild, which simplifies the process of building and installing modules, as well as detailed documentation provided through resources such as the Linux Kernel Documentation project. This extensive support encourages new contributors to engage with kernel development, contributing their own modular enhancements and becoming a part of the wider community.

In conclusion, the modular nature of the Linux kernel represents a foundational principle that enhances flexibility, performance, and community involvement in the operating system. The ability to dynamically load and unload modules, combined with a clear separation of responsibilities and extensive community collaboration, fosters an environment where innovation thrives. As technology continues to evolve, the modular architecture of Linux will remain instrumental in adapting to new challenges and optimizing system performance across a diverse landscape of use cases. Understanding this modularity is crucial for anyone looking to delve deeper into the realm of Linux kernel development, reflecting the collaborative spirit and shared ownership that continues to drive this powerful operating system forward.

4.3. The Role of Init Systems

In the architecture of the Linux operating system, init systems play a pivotal role by managing the initialization and configuration of the system during the boot process and maintaining services during runtime. An init system serves as the first process started by the kernel during system booting. Its primary responsibilities include starting and managing system services, ensuring the system is in a stable state, and coordinating the various system components necessary for the operating system to function effectively.

Historically, the init system has evolved through several iterations, reflecting the changing needs and complexities of modern computing environments. The traditional init system for UNIX systems is the classic System V init, a simple, linear approach where services are started in a predefined order through a series of shell scripts located in init directories. While System V init had the advantage of simplicity, its limitations became clear as system complexity grew. The sequential nature of service starts could lead to longer boot times and issues related to service dependencies—one service might fail to start if another it depended on was not available.

As computing demands increased, alternative init systems were developed to address these limitations, introducing more sophisticated dependency management, improved parallelism, and better service control. Foremost among these was the introduction of Upstart, which offered an event-driven framework, allowing services to be started or stopped in response to events, significantly enhancing boot performance and responsiveness.

However, the most prominent and widely adopted init system in contemporary Linux distributions is systemd. Developed by Lennart Poettering and others, systemd represents a paradigm shift in how init systems function. Built around the concept of units, systemd allows for an advanced dependency management framework ensuring services are started in parallel, facilitating much faster boot times and resource utilization. Units can be services, sockets, devices, mounts, and more—a flexible system that captures the various elements necessary for a modern computing environment. With systemd, developers can define services in unit files, which provide detailed configuration parameters such as dependencies, resource limits, and execution conditions.

One of the pioneering features of systemd is its ability to manage services using the concept of "socket activation". This method leverages network sockets, allowing services to start only when they are needed—essentially eliminating unused resource consumption. The management of services via cgroups also allows for resource limiting and prioritization of service dependencies, ensuring critical services receive the necessary resources to operate effectively.

Another key aspect of systemd is its centralized logging strategy provided by journalctl, which aggregates and manages log data across all system components, enabling easy troubleshooting and monitoring. The logging framework allows logs to be accessed in real-time, streamlining diagnostics for administrators facing service failures or performance issues.

Systemd also supports user-level services, allowing individual users to create and manage their own services without requiring root privileges. This is an empowering feature for developers and users, as it allows them to run applications and respond to events that are specific to their needs without impacting the system-wide services governed by the root user.

Despite its advantages, systemd has generated controversy within the Linux community due to its complexity and the degree of control it exerts over the system. Some advocates of traditional init systems argue that systemd introduces unnecessary complexity, shifting the focus from the modularity and simplicity that many users prefer. Critics contend that this monolithic approach can lead to complications in debugging and managing services independently.

Furthermore, various alternative init systems have bolstered the ecosystem, such as OpenRC, runit, and S6. These systems promote a philosophy that emphasizes simplicity, modularity, and adherence to the UNIX principle of designing small, single-purpose components that perform well together. While these alternatives may not achieve the level of widespread adoption seen with systemd, they maintain a loyal user base and emphasize different design perspectives, reflecting the diversity of philosophies present in the open-source community.

The role of init systems extends beyond mere service management; it lays the foundation for how systems boot, configure, and manage resources throughout their operational lifespan. An efficient init system is crucial for optimizing performance while providing reliable service management, directly impacting user experiences and system stability.

In today's landscape, where virtualization and containerization play key roles, init systems must also adapt to the requirements of these environments. For example, container orchestrators like Docker leverage the principles behind traditional init systems to manage container lifecycles, thus emphasizing the importance of service management in various application deployment paradigms.

In summary, init systems have evolved significantly from their traditional implementations, driven by the increasing complexity of modern computing demands. The advancements represented by systems like systemd highlight the shift towards efficient service management, parallel execution, and centralized logging, while also reflecting the ongoing debates within the community about the balance between simplicity and feature richness. As developers continue to innovate and adapt Linux to meet future challenges, the role of init systems remains vital to sustaining performance, service reliability, and effective resource management across diverse computing environments.

4.4. Boot Process: From BIOS to Kernel

Booting a Linux system is a multi-step process that starts long before the operating system itself begins to load. From the moment you power on your computer to when the Linux kernel takes control, a series of critical steps must occur to ensure that the system initializes properly. This process, which plays a vital role in the overall functionality of the operating system, can be broken down into several key components, beginning with the Basic Input/Output System (BIOS) or Unified Extensible Firmware Interface (UEFI) and culminating with the loading of the kernel.

The process initiates when the power button is pressed, causing the system's power supply to activate. This triggers the BIOS or UEFI firmware, which resides on the motherboard. The BIOS is a legacy system, stored in ROM or flash memory, that has been the backbone of the boot process for many years. UEFI, on the other hand, is a modern alternative to BIOS, designed to overcome several limitations of its predecessor, including support for larger hard drives and faster boot times. Regardless of which one is employed, the subsequent steps are largely similar.

Once activated, the BIOS/UEFI performs POST (Power-On Self-Test) checks. This critical diagnostic phase verifies that the computer's essential hardware components—such as the CPU, memory, and storage devices—are functioning correctly. If any issues are detected, the BIOS typically emits a series of beep codes or displays error messages, allowing users to diagnose hardware failures before proceeding further. A successful POST indicates that the system is ready to initialize its hardware components.

Following POST, the BIOS/UEFI looks for a boot device, a process set in the firmware's configuration. The boot device could be a hard disk, solid-state drive, USB drive, or even a network source, depending on system settings. The firmware reads the boot sector of the selected device to locate the bootloader. The bootloader is a small program that plays a vital role in the boot process by preparing the operating system's kernel for execution.

The most commonly used bootloaders in Linux systems are GRUB (GRand Unified Bootloader) and LILO (LInux LOader). GRUB is particularly versatile and widely adopted due to its ability to support multiple operating systems and configurations. Once the BIOS or UEFI identifies the correct bootloader, it transfers control to this program.

Upon execution, the bootloader's primary task is to load the kernel into memory. It does so by retrieving the kernel image, typically compressed, from the designated boot partition. GRUB provides a menu interface where users can select which operating system or kernel to boot, particularly useful in dual-boot or multi-boot scenarios. Importantly, this stage of the boot process also allows for kernel parameters —additional instructions that can modify the kernel's behavior during startup—to be defined.

Once the kernel image is loaded into memory, the bootloader then loads the initial RAM disk (initrd or initramfs). This temporary filesystem contains essential drivers and modules required by the kernel to mount the actual root filesystem. Since the kernel needs to access storage devices and other hardware components before it can transition fully to the root filesystem, this step provides the necessary tools for that initial disk access. The initrd/initramfs plays a critical role, particularly in systems that require specific drivers to boot, ensuring that the kernel has the means to access the disk where the operating system resides.

Following the successful loading of the kernel and initramfs, the bootloader transfers control to the kernel itself, initiating the kernel's initialization process. At this stage, the kernel initializes hardware components, sets up memory management, and begins to configure system resources. It loads all necessary kernel modules (if any) that were specified during the boot process.

The kernel then mounts the root filesystem, making it accessible for the operating system. This transition marks an essential point: the kernel is now in control of all core aspects of the system. Once the kernel successfully mounts the root filesystem, it looks for the init process, traditionally located at /sbin/init. The init process is the first user-space application that the kernel executes, setting the stage for further initialization of system services and user interfaces.

From this point on, the init process—often supplanted by advanced init systems such as systemd or Upstart—manages the remaining startup tasks. It initializes system services and other daemons essential for the operation of user-space applications and the operating system as a whole. This could involve starting networking services, loading user interfaces, managing security protocols, and many other functions aimed at ensuring that the system is stable, responsive, and ready for user interaction.

Throughout this entire boot process, several checks, configurations, and confirmations take place to ensure that all components are functioning cohesively. Each step depends on the successful completion of the previous one, illustrating the complexity and interconnectedness of modern operating systems.

Ultimately, the journey from BIOS/UEFI to kernel control is a fascinating interplay of hardware, firmware, and software, each step precisely orchestrated to ensure that users are greeted with a functioning operating system. Understanding this process empowers users and developers alike to troubleshoot boot issues, optimize system performance, and appreciate the intricacies of system initialization that lay the groundwork for everything users experience in their interactions with Linux. As we reflect on the boot process, we recognize its importance not just in enabling the kernel to take control but in serving as the gateway to all functionalities that the Linux operating system has to offer.

4.5. Securing the Kernel: Best Practices

In the realm of operating system security, securing the kernel stands as one of the most critical aspects of maintaining the integrity and stability of the entire system. The kernel serves as the core interface between the hardware and the software, facilitating resource management, process scheduling, and device interactions. Consequently, any vulnerabilities or weaknesses in the kernel can bring catastrophic consequences—not only for the operating system but also for the applications and services that rely on it. Therefore, adopting best practices for kernel security is paramount for developers, system administrators, and organizations that use Linux across various environments.

One of the foundational practices for securing the kernel begins with a robust understanding of its architecture and capabilities. Developers should familiarize themselves with the kernel's security features, including access control mechanisms, security modules, and the use of namespaces and cgroups. These built-in features can help enforce security policies and isolate resources, thereby minimizing the attack surface. The Linux kernel employs a range of access control models, such as Discretionary Access Control (DAC) and Mandatory Access Control (MAC), which can restrict user access to files and processes based on their permissions and roles.

Kernel developers should also prioritize code quality and security by following secure coding practices. This involves rigorous vetting of code contributions to detect and eliminate vulnerabilities before they make their way into the mainline kernel. Utilizing static and dynamic analysis tools can help identify potential security issues at the code level, while integrated development environments equipped with linters can enforce coding standards to promote consistency and clarity. Employing pair programming or code reviews among experienced developers can also provide critical insights, fostering an environment of learning and expertise sharing.

In addition to following secure coding practices, testing and validation play vital roles in securing the kernel. Continuous integration and automated testing frameworks are instrumental in ensuring that new patches and features do not introduce vulnerabilities. Kernel developers can implement unit tests, regression tests, and fuzz testing to identify unexpected behaviors or security flaws. Keeping the kernel and all its components up-to-date with the latest security patches is equally essential, as vulnerabilities are continuously discovered and addressed by the community. Organizations must establish policies for promptly applying security updates while maintaining thorough testing to ensure that these updates do not compromise system stability.

Managing user permissions and ensuring that only trusted and necessary components run in kernel space is a critical aspect of securing the kernel. Developers should adhere to the principle of least privilege, which suggests that processes should operate with the minimum level of permissions necessary to perform their tasks. Administrators can utilize tools like SELinux or AppArmor to enforce security policies that confine applications, ensuring that even if exploited, their access to critical system resources remains limited. The implementation of these security frameworks can significantly reduce the likelihood of privilege escalation attacks, where a malicious actor seeks to gain higher permissions than intended.

In the event of a breach or vulnerability, it is crucial to have incident response protocols ready. Organizations must equip their teams with the tools needed to monitor kernel behavior actively and analyze logs for anomalous activities. Utilizing tools such as audit daemon logs, syslog, and tools for real-time monitoring can help detect security incidents as they happen. Responding quickly to any detected anomalies ensures mitigation of potential threats before they escalate into more severe issues.

Another significant facet of kernel security involves hardening the kernel environment. Kernel hardening techniques aim to strengthen the operating system against potential attacks. This includes compiling the kernel with security features like stack canaries, address space layout randomization (ASLR), and kernel module signing. Each of these mechanisms creates additional hurdles for potential attackers, making it harder for them to exploit vulnerabilities or execute arbitrary code within the kernel. Developers can also take advantage of the "CONFIG_HARDENED_USERCOPY" and "CONFIG_STRICT_DEVMEM" options during kernel configuration to tightly control memory access and allocation.

Additionally, organizations and developers should be mindful of their use of third-party kernel modules. Modules can extend kernel functionality, but they can also introduce security risks if not reviewed carefully. Hence, developers should thoroughly vet any third-party modules for security compliance and, where possible, prefer using modules that are actively maintained within the kernel community. Utilizing the Linux kernel's native module functionality, as opposed to user-installed modules, often comes with added security benefits and community support.

Alongside traditional kernel security practices, the adoption of a security-focused development lifecycle is essential. This involves integrating security measures throughout the entire development process, from design to deployment. Engaging with the community and staying abreast of ongoing security discussions, vulnerabilities being discovered, and new best practices being introduced is crucial for developers involved in the kernel space. Participating in conferences, summits, and forums focused on Linux kernel security can help drive collaborative efforts towards enhancing kernel security.

Lastly, organizations should consider using security-focused distributions tailored for mission-critical applications and environments, especially where security is paramount. Distributions like Qubes OS or Alpine Linux emphasize a security-first approach and often come with hardened configurations and tools that help manage risk at every level. By deploying secure distributions, organizations can further safeguard their systems and leverage the expertise embedded in these specially designed environments.

In conclusion, securing the Linux kernel requires a comprehensive approach that encompasses sound coding practices, active monitoring, hardening techniques, user privilege management, and continuous engagement with the community. By implementing these best practices, developers and administrators can significantly reduce the risk of security vulnerabilities, ensuring the integrity and availability of their systems. As threats continue to evolve, maintaining vigilance and a proactive stance toward kernel security will be indispensable to the resilience and longevity of Linux as a platform for modern computing. The ongoing collaboration within the kernel community and the cultivation of security-first thinking among developers will undoubtedly be pivotal in shaping the future of Linux security strategies.

5. Kernel Development Process

5.1. Contribution Guidelines and Ethics

In the world of open-source software, the contributions of individuals and organizations largely shape the growth and direction of projects, especially one as significant as the Linux kernel. Understanding the contribution guidelines and ethics surrounding kernel development is critical for maintaining an inclusive, productive, and high-quality collaborative environment. This subchapter will detail the various aspects that guide contributions to the Linux kernel, explore the ethical considerations involved, and underscore the importance of community participation.

At the core of the contribution guidelines is the principle of creating a cohesive and reliable software product. The Linux kernel, which serves as the foundation for countless distributions and applications, requires a rigorous development process that emphasizes quality, performance, and security. Therefore, contributors must adhere to specific coding standards and practices established by the kernel maintainers. These standards include clear documentation, consistent styles, and effective testing measures to ensure that submitted patches and code alterations enhance, rather than undermine, the kernel's capabilities.

One of the primary means of contributing to the Linux kernel is through patch submissions. Patches must be created using the `git format-patch` command and submitted for review to the appropriate kernel mailing list. This process underscores the importance of communication within the development community. Mailing lists serve not only as repositories for code discussions but also as open platforms for developers to exchange ideas, offer critiques, and assist one another in refining their contributions. Each patch submission invites scrutiny; developers are expected to present their work clearly and justify the need for changes, fostering a culture of collective responsibility and peer review.

Before submitting patches, contributions must undergo thorough self-review and testing to validate their functionality and ensure they adhere to the kernel's established coding standards. The Linux kernel has a wealth of documentation, including the kernel coding style guide, which delineates guidelines on formatting and source code arrangements. Adhering to these guidelines not only streamlines the review process but also reflects a contributor's commitment to maintaining code integrity and coherence.

The kernel's maintainers play a crucial role in overseeing the contribution process. Each subsystem within the kernel typically has designated maintainers, individuals responsible for reviewing incoming submissions pertinent to their areas of expertise. This structure helps handle the volume of contributions while maintaining high standards for quality. Contributors are encouraged to engage with maintainers to seek advice, solicit feedback, and clarify any uncertainties regarding submission processes.

Beyond technical aspects, ethical considerations are paramount in the Linux kernel community. The ethos of open source is deeply rooted in values such as collaboration, transparency, and mutual respect among contributors. This culture promotes an environment where diverse voices can contribute to shaping the software. New contributors, in particular, should be met with encouragement and support, as they represent the lifeblood of ongoing innovation within the project. Experienced developers are often urged to mentor newcomers, guiding them through the intricacies of the contribution process, providing feedback on their submissions, and fostering an atmosphere conducive to learning and growth.

Moreover, ethical considerations extend to the need for inclusivity in the kernel development community. Acknowledging the contributions of individuals from diverse backgrounds is crucial for fostering a vibrant ecosystem while ensuring that all voices are heard. The Linux community places significant emphasis on diversity initiatives, and contributors should be mindful of inclusive language and practices that remove barriers to participation. Respectful communication, along with constructive critiques that help amplify the strengths of others, is essential for nurturing a supportive and welcoming community.

Security is another critical ethical facet of kernel contributions. Contributors must abide by best practices to maximize security and minimize vulnerabilities. This includes adhering to secure coding standards to mitigate issues such as buffer overflows or race conditions. Transparency about potential concerns and being diligent in reporting vulnerabilities strengthens the overall stability of the kernel, promoting a culture of accountability and trust.

In addition to direct contributions to the codebase, engaged participation in discussions surrounding design decisions and feature proposals is valued. The kernel community encourages debates that emphasize well-articulated viewpoints, with technical justifications rather than personal opinions. This collaborative model fosters comprehensive decision-making, where contributions can ultimately guide the kernel's evolution while reflecting the collective wisdom of the community.

Engaging with the community through various forums and actively participating in kernel events, conferences, and summits can also deepen a contributor's involvement. These gatherings allow for networking, sharing experiences, and discussing pivotal issues within the kernel space, facilitating collaborative efforts to address challenges.

Furthermore, adherence to licensing norms and understanding the legal implications of contributions is essential for participants in the kernel development process. The Linux kernel is released under the GNU General Public License (GPL), which governs how the software can be used, modified, and distributed. Contributors must ensure that their submissions remain compliant with these licensing terms, thereby preserving the integrity of the open-source framework upon which the kernel relies.

In summary, the contribution guidelines and ethics surrounding Linux kernel development are a tapestry woven with principles of quality, inclusivity, respect, and security. As contributors navigate the complexities of patch submissions and code enhancements, they embody the spirit of collaboration that has driven the kernel's success. By prioritizing quality, mentoring others, fostering inclusivity, maintaining security, and remaining engaged with the community, contributors can ensure that they uphold the ideals of an open-source ecosystem while helping guide the evolution of one of the most significant projects in the world of computing. As each developer continues to contribute their skills and knowledge, the kernel community flourishes, propelling the advancement of technology forward, one collaborative effort at a time.

5.2. Understanding Kernel Mailing Lists

In the world of Linux kernel development, kernel mailing lists are vital communication channels that facilitate collaboration, discussion, and knowledge sharing among developers, contributors, and enthusiasts. These mailing lists serve not only as forums for technical discussions regarding the kernel's architecture, features, and bugs, but also as platforms for community-building and collective decision-making. Understanding the purpose and functioning of these mailing lists is crucial for anyone looking to engage meaningfully with the Linux kernel community.

Kernel mailing lists have a longstanding historical significance, tracing back to the early days of Linux development. Initially, Linus Torvalds and a handful of developers utilized mailing lists to debate the merits of various features and resolve issues, paving the way for an inclusive and open-source developmental ethos. In this tradition, several established mailing lists have emerged, each fulfilling specific roles within the ecosystem.

The most prominent kernel mailing list is the "linux-kernel" list, which serves as the primary forum for discussions related to the Linux kernel itself. Developers post patches for review, seek advice on technical matters, announce new features, and report bugs or issues they've encountered. The traffic on this list can be quite high, given the robust and diverse community of contributors spanning various backgrounds and expertise levels. New contributors are encouraged to engage by introducing themselves and sharing their intentions, as fostering familiarity within the community plays an essential role in building collaborative relationships.

In addition to the primary linux-kernel list, there are several subsystem-specific mailing lists, each dedicated to particular areas of the kernel, such as networking (netdev), file systems (linux-fsdevel), memory management (linux-mm), and many others. These focused lists allow developers who specialize in certain subsystems to discuss enhancements, address bugs, and share relevant insights pertinent to their specific domains. Engaging on these specialized lists can facilitate targeted discussions that yield concrete contributions to the kernel.

One of the core functions of kernel mailing lists is the patch review process. When developers create modifications or enhancements to the kernel, they generate patches that catalog their changes. These patches are submitted to the relevant mailing lists, inviting feedback from fellow developers. The review process serves multiple purposes —it ensures code quality, maintains coding standards, and enables collective knowledge sharing to identify any unintended consequences of the changes. This collaborative evaluation helps improve the end product, as concerns and suggestions are surfaced in an open forum.

Getting effective feedback on patches typically entails adhering to specific guidelines established by the kernel community. For example, patch submissions should include clear commit messages, concise explanations detailing the need for the change, and accompanying code comments to enhance the clarity of what the changes entail. These practices facilitate efficient reviews and foster productive discussions. Developers often refer to the "SubmittingPatches" document, which provides detailed instructions for structuring submissions and enhancing the likelihood of acceptance.

The kernel mailing lists also serve as a repository for knowledge and best practices. Through discussions and archived threads, developers can access valuable insights regarding the intricacies of kernel development, common pitfalls, and effective debugging approaches. The ability to search historical discussions provides an educational resource for newcomers, allowing them to benefit from seasoned contributors' experiences.

In addition to technical discussions, the kernel mailing lists function as platforms for higher-level conversations regarding the evolution of the Linux kernel as a whole. This includes discussions on release cycles, proposed changes in governance, feature requests, and strategic decisions that affect the community at large. By hearing diverse opinions, the community can arrive at consensus decisions that reflect the collective interests of its members.

An essential aspect of kernel mailing lists is the culture within which they operate. The community generally values respectful and constructive dialogue, emphasizing the importance of fostering an inclusive and welcoming environment. Contributors are encouraged to be patient, helpful, and supportive, particularly towards newcomers who are just starting their journey in kernel development. Maintaining this cooperative spirit is paramount in ensuring that all voices are heard and appreciated.

However, the community does face challenges in sustaining effective communication. Given the breadth of discussions, there's a risk of information overload, leaving less experienced developers feeling intimidated or overwhelmed. Thus, it is vital for community members to actively cultivate support networks and mentorship dynamics where newcomers can be guided smoothly through this ocean of information.

Additionally, etiquette plays a significant role in kernel mailing lists. Developers are expected to utilize proper formatting in their communications, including subject lines that accurately reflect the content of their messages. It's crucial to retain clarity and relevance, providing context for discussions and ensuring that threads remain focused. Adhering to these standards promotes an organized structure and enhances the overall community experience.

In conclusion, understanding kernel mailing lists within the Linux kernel ecosystem offers a glimpse into the collaborative spirit that fuels its development. These mailing lists serve as central hubs for communication, enabling developers to share patches, engage in discussions, and collectively contribute to the evolution of the kernel. By navigating this space according to established guidelines and fostering a supportive culture, contributors can help propel the Linux kernel forward while simultaneously enriching their own expertise and experience within the broader community. Embracing this environment enables the steady exchange of knowledge, an essential feature of the open-source paradigm, which continues to nurture innovation and diversity in the world of technology.

5.3. Version Control with Git

Version control is an essential aspect of modern software development, and in the context of the Linux kernel, it plays a pivotal role in managing the complexity, collaboration, and continuous evolution of this monumental project. Git, developed by Linus Torvalds himself in 2005, has become the de facto system for version control in the Linux kernel community, providing powerful and efficient tools to manage changes in the codebase. Understanding how to effectively utilize Git in kernel development can enhance collaboration, ensure code integrity, and facilitate ongoing innovation.

At its core, Git is a distributed version control system that enables multiple developers to work concurrently on the same codebase without hindering each other's progress. This is particularly important in a global project like the Linux kernel, where contributions may come from thousands of developers operating in diverse environments. Git allows developers to create branches, which are independent lines of development that can be merged back into the main branch after changes have been reviewed and validated. This branching strategy fosters an environment where experimentation and innovation can thrive, as developers have the freedom to implement new features or fix bugs without the risk of immediately affecting the stable kernel.

One of the primary commands used in Git is `git clone`, which enables developers to create a local copy of the kernel's main repository (usually hosted on platforms like GitHub or kernel.org). This local repository allows contributors to make changes and test their modifications freely. After making changes, developers can use `git add` to stage specific files for inclusion in the next commit, followed by `git commit`, where they provide a message that describes their changes. Commit messages are critically important; following the kernel's conventions, they should be concise yet descriptive, helping maintainers understand the purpose and context of the submitted changes.

The process of contributing to the Linux kernel typically involves several steps. After making and committing changes locally, developers create a new branch for their work using `git checkout -b feature-branch`, where "feature-branch" is a user-defined name for the branch. Once modifications are tested successfully, they can be pushed to a remote repository using `git push`. This step prepares the changes for submission through the kernel's patch submission process.

The kernel community leverages the functionality of Git to manage patches effectively. A common practice involves using the `git format-patch` command, which generates a series of patch files corresponding to the commits made by a developer. These patch files can then be sent to the relevant kernel mailing lists for review. The reviewing process is essential to maintain the overall quality and stability of the kernel; maintainers will critique contributions, ask for changes, and discuss the best approaches to integrate new code.

In tandem with Git's feature set, the kernel community emphasizes the importance of clear and thorough communication during the contribution process. Patches should include context about what the changes are intended to solve, the rationale behind the modifications, and any potential impacts. This transparency facilitates productive discussions among contributors and maintainers, driving collective decision-making and reinforcing the collaborative spirit of open-source development.

Moreover, Git's branching model aligns perfectly with the kernel's development workflow. The Linux kernel follows a structured release cycle, characterized by a mainline branch that progresses towards stable releases. New features and major changes are initially developed in separate branches, allowing maintainers to integrate smaller, well-defined enhancements into the stable mainline branch without interrupting its continuity. This results in several development branches, each focusing on different goals—some may target experimental features while others remain dedicated to bug fixes and optimizations.

As kernel development continues to evolve, Git enables efficient management of backports—a crucial aspect of maintaining stability across different kernel versions used in various distributions. Backporting refers to the practice of taking newer features or fixes from the latest kernel version and applying them to older versions. Using Git, developers can cherry-pick commits from the main branch and integrate them into the appropriate stable branches, ensuring that both legacy systems and users running older distributions can benefit from the latest improvements.

The collaborative environment nurtured by Git extends beyond individual contributions. It fosters a culture of mentorship and shared knowledge. Experienced developers often take the time to review and provide feedback on newer contributors' patches, helping them to improve their coding skills and understand the nuances of kernel development. By leveraging tools such as `git bisect`, developers can efficiently identify when a bug was introduced by narrowing down through commit history, facilitating quicker resolutions and enhancing the overall robustness of the kernel.

In addition to the standard Git commands, many kernel developers make use of shell scripts and custom tooling to streamline their workflows. These utilities can automate repetitive tasks, perform linting and static analysis on changes, and facilitate submission processes, all of which contribute to smoother development cycles and reduced overhead.

In summary, version control with Git is fundamental to the Linux kernel's development process, enabling collaboration, quality assurance, and efficient management of changes across a vast and diverse contributor base. By leveraging Git effectively, developers can navigate the complexities of kernel development, ensuring that their contributions align with the kernel's rigorous standards. As the community continues to grow and evolve, mastering Git will remain an essential skill for anyone looking to contribute to the ever-expanding tapestry of the Linux kernel, strengthening its legacy as one of the most influential open-source projects in history. The synergy between Git and the kernel community encapsulates the essence of collaborative software development, where diverse voices unite to forge a robust, resilient, and dynamic future in computing.

5.4. Testing and Debugging Techniques

Testing and debugging are critical components in the development cycle of the Linux kernel, reflecting the rigor and complexity involved in managing such a sophisticated piece of software that serves as the backbone for numerous systems and applications. This chapter delves into the various techniques, tools, and best practices for testing and debugging within the Linux kernel environment, emphasizing the importance of maintaining code quality, reliability, and performance.

At its core, testing in the Linux kernel context refers to the processes that ensure new features, bug fixes, and enhancements function correctly and do not introduce new issues. Given the vast scope of the kernel and its impact across different hardware architectures and use cases, a comprehensive approach to testing is imperative. Unlike traditional application testing, kernel testing contends with lower-level interactions with the hardware, making it essential to adopt specialized methods tailored to the unique challenges posed by kernel development.

One prominent technique for kernel testing is regression testing, which aims to identify whether recent changes to the codebase have adversely affected existing functionality. This method typically involves a suite of automated test cases that cover various aspects of the kernel, including file systems, memory management, memory locking, and scheduling. The Kernel CI (Continuous Integration) project exemplifies efforts in this domain, utilizing a combination of real-world hardware and virtualization to run a wide array of tests on kernel changes regularly. When a contributor submits a patch, automated testing systems validate the code against these predefined test cases, helping catch regressions early in the development process.

Another common testing technique involves the use of unit tests, which focus on individual components of the kernel, ensuring that each piece performs as expected in isolation. Unit testing frameworks like the Kernel Testing Framework provide developers with tools to write and execute tests targeting specific functions or modules. By exercising precise code sections, developers can validate that new changes align with the intended functionality and do not introduce unforeseen side effects.

Integration testing, on the other hand, assesses how well different components of the kernel interact with one another once separate modules are combined. This type of testing is critical for a system as interconnected as the Linux kernel. Various tools enable developers to simulate complex scenarios where they can monitor the system's behavior under specific conditions, ensuring that components such as the memory management subsystem interact correctly with process scheduling mechanisms.

Furthermore, the kernel employs the use of performance testing to evaluate how efficiently the kernel operates under different workloads and system configurations. With tools such as "perf" and "ftrace", developers can profile kernel code to analyze performance bottlenecks and resource usage. These profiling capabilities are essential for understanding the behavior of the kernel, allowing developers to optimize critical paths in the code that impact overall system performance.

Debugging the kernel represents its own set of challenges due to its low-level nature and the potential for system crashes or hangs when errors occur. Kernel developers utilize various debugging techniques that cater to the specific requirements of kernel code. The primary toolset for debugging includes printk statements, which allow developers to output messages to the kernel log. By strategically placing printk statements throughout the code, developers can track the execution flow and variable values during runtime.

For more complex debugging scenarios, kernel developers turn to the Kernel Debugger (KGDB), which provides a means of debugging the kernel in a live environment. KGDB allows engineers to attach a debugger to a running kernel instance via a serial port or Ethernet connection, enabling them to step through code and inspect memory while the system operates. This level of insight is invaluable for diagnosing elusive bugs that surface in production environments.

Dynamic debugging is another significant aspect of kernel debugging. The Dynamic Debugging Framework allows developers to enable or disable specific debugging messages at runtime without requiring a recompilation of the kernel. This flexibility is particularly valuable in live systems, where developers can react to issues promptly without disrupting service.

In terms of addressing specific issues, the approach to debugging must be systematic and informed by the principles of good software development. The analysis of kernel panics—situations where the kernel encounters an unrecoverable error and shuts down—requires developers to examine panic messages, stack traces, and the conditions leading up to the panic. Tools like "crash" allow developers to analyze core dumps produced during panics, offering an opportunity to inspect the state of the kernel at the time of failure.

Aside from these techniques, the kernel community readily engages in peer reviews and collaboration to ensure high-quality code submission. By employing code review practices, experienced developers help identify potential bugs or design flaws in submitted patches before they become part of the main kernel codebase. This collaborative effort strengthens the overall integrity of the kernel and fosters mentorship for newer developers.

Essentially, effective testing and debugging require a diverse mix of techniques tailored specifically for the kernel environment alongside the backgrounds of its contributors. Key to productive testing and debugging practices is the culture of thoroughness and responsiveness cultivated within the kernel community, where collaborative spirit encourages ongoing improvements and innovation.

Finally, continuous education and knowledge sharing stand as cornerstones of successful kernel testing and debugging practices. Developers are encouraged to document the processes, share successes and failures, and collaborate within forums such as the Linux Kernel Mailing List or communication platforms to nurture learning among peers. By fostering an environment where collective knowledge thrives, developers contribute not only to the stability and performance of the Linux kernel but also to the larger ethos of open-source collaboration that defines the Linux community.

In summary, testing and debugging techniques specific to the Linux kernel reflect a blend of rigor, creativity, and collaboration. Emphasizing automated testing, performance profiling, strategic debugging, peer reviews, and active community engagement, kernel developers ensure that the kernel remains robust, efficient, and capable of supporting the myriad applications that rely upon it. Understanding and mastering these techniques is essential for anyone involved in kernel development, protecting the core of Linux and fostering a culture of excellence that resonates throughout the ecosystem it supports.

5.5. Code Review and Mentoring New Developers

In the realm of software development, particularly within the context of the Linux kernel, the processes of code review and mentoring play an indispensable role in fostering a robust, collaborative, and innovative community. As contributors join forces to enhance the kernel, it is crucial to ensure that new developers not only learn the intricacies of kernel programming but also understand the expectations, culture, and best practices inherent in this unique environment. This chapter explores the significance of code review and mentorship, highlighting how they contribute to the kernel's success and how they can be effectively approached within the community.

Code review is vital for maintaining the quality and stability of the Linux kernel. Given its complexity and the critical nature of the systems it runs, rigorous code review practices help prevent bugs, security vulnerabilities, and performance issues from making their way into the main codebase. When a developer submits a patch, it undergoes scrutiny from experienced maintainers and peers to ensure it aligns with the kernel's standards. This evaluation process serves several important functions, including identifying potential pitfalls in logic, assessing the impact of proposed changes on existing functionalities, and ensuring adherence to established coding guidelines.

A well-conducted code review process cultivates a culture of excellence and learning. Reviewers provide constructive feedback, suggesting improvements and emphasizing best practices related to coding style, documentation, and testing. This engagement allows contributors, especially newcomers, to gain insights into the kernel's design principles and the rationale behind various decisions. As they absorb this knowledge, their skills develop, and they become more attuned to the expectations and intricacies of working with the Linux kernel.

For new developers, mentorship emerges as a powerful tool for navigating the complexities of kernel development. The kernel community thrives on collaboration, and seasoned contributors often take the initiative to guide less experienced developers. This mentorship can manifest in various ways, including one-on-one discussions, technical writing, shared coding sessions, and participation in mailing lists. Mentorship helps to demystify the development process, provides targeted guidance on optimizing code, and fosters a sense of belonging within the community.

One of the early challenges faced by newcomers is understanding the kernel's complex architecture and its various subsystems. A mentor can offer valuable insights into how different parts of the kernel interact, helping new developers appreciate the overall structure and purpose of various components. Additionally, mentors can introduce new contributors to important resources—documentation, coding standards, and testing frameworks—that will prove indispensable as they embark on their journey in kernel development.

As the Linux kernel is shaped by contributions from individuals and organizations across the globe, it is essential for mentors to embrace an inclusive and welcoming approach. Encouraging diversity and actively involving contributors from different backgrounds enriches the kernel community and promotes innovative thinking. This commitment to inclusivity is reflected in the kernel's culture, where contributions are valued based on their quality rather than the stature of the contributors. Mentors play a crucial role in creating a supportive environment that celebrates the unique perspectives and ideas of every participant.

Moreover, mentorship extends beyond technical instruction; it also encompasses professional development for new developers. Mentors can help fledgling contributors set goals, navigate their learning paths, and explore career trajectories within the open-source ecosystem. By encouraging participation in conferences, workshops, and other community events, mentors foster opportunities for networking and further learning, ensuring that new developers have the resources and connections needed to thrive.

Encouraging participation in review processes also helps new developers build confidence in their abilities. By involving them in discussions and decision-making around code changes, mentors allow newcomers to express their thoughts and contributions. This engagement not only strengthens their understanding of the development processes but also cultivates ownership of their work, leading to a deeper commitment to the kernel community.

It is important to remember that code review and mentoring are not one-sided processes. While experienced developers impart knowledge, they can also learn from the insights and fresh perspectives offered by newcomers. This reciprocal relationship fosters an atmosphere of continuous learning and collaboration, where every contributor—regardless of experience—can have a meaningful impact on the project.

As a practical approach to embedding code review and mentorship into the kernel development process, several strategies can be employed. Organizations and project maintainers can establish formal mentorship programs that match newcomers with experienced developers, ensuring that every new contributor has a path to seek guidance. Additionally, incorporating formalized review processes with clear milestones can help streamline the contribution journey, making it easier for newcomers to navigate.

Furthermore, the kernel community can benefit from fostering an environment where constructive feedback is valued and mistakes are viewed as learning opportunities. Many experienced developers have made their share of errors during their time in kernel development, and sharing these experiences can demystify the process while encouraging newcomers to persevere. Recognizing that everyone is on a continuous journey of growth helps cultivate an environment grounded in encouragement and support.

In conclusion, the interplay between code review and mentoring in the Linux kernel community serves to strengthen the quality of contributions while fostering a collaborative and inclusive atmosphere. By implementing effective review processes and investing in the mentorship of new developers, the community not only enhances the kernel's robustness and stability but also nurtures the next generation of innovators and contributors. As new voices join the chorus of kernel development, they carry with them the potential for fresh ideas and solutions that will further propel the evolution of this remarkable open-source project. Through ongoing support and collective effort, the Linux kernel community will continue to thrive, ensuring its place at the forefront of technology and collaboration in the modern computing landscape.

6. The Kernel Community and Ecosystem

6.1. The Linux Foundation: Role and Influence

The Linux Foundation serves as a pivotal organization within the ecosystem surrounding the Linux kernel, playing a multifaceted role in supporting its development and growth. Established in 2000, the foundation aims to promote, protect, and advance the Linux operating system and its popularization across diverse applications and industries. The influence of the Linux Foundation is far-reaching, impacting not only kernel development but also the broader open-source community and technological advancements globally.

One of the primary functions of the Linux Foundation is to provide infrastructure and resources for kernel development. It facilitates collaboration among developers, companies, and organizations that rely on Linux, offering a neutral ground where all stakeholders can contribute to the common goals of enhancing kernel features, addressing security vulnerabilities, and improving performance. Through its support, the foundation enables the continuous evolution of the Linux kernel, ensuring it remains a leading choice for operating systems worldwide.

Membership in the Linux Foundation encompasses a wide range of entities, including major technology companies, startups, educational institutions, and individuals. This diversity represents a rich tapestry of expertise and innovation, drawing a collaborative ecosystem where shared knowledge thrives. Members like IBM, Intel, Google, and Microsoft have made significant contributions to kernel development, bringing with them extensive resources, talent, and infrastructure that fuel advancements in open-source software.

The Linux Foundation also organizes crucial events, such as the annual Linux Kernel Summit and various developer conferences. These gatherings provide an opportunity for kernel developers, maintainers, and contributors to meet in person, discuss advancements, share experiences, and forge partnerships. Such face-to-face interactions accelerate collaboration, allowing parties to align on priorities and address challenges collectively.

In addition to community-building efforts, the Linux Foundation champions educational initiatives aimed at nurturing the next generation of developers and engineers. It sponsors training programs, workshops, and certification courses designed to equip individuals with the skills needed to contribute effectively to the kernel and navigate the complexities of open-source software development. Through such initiatives, the foundation helps cultivate new talent, ensuring that the Linux kernel continues to benefit from fresh ideas and perspectives.

Beyond its central role within the kernel community, the Linux Foundation actively participates in advocating for open-source software more broadly. It raises awareness of the importance of open-source principles, promoting transparency, collaboration, and user freedom as critical tenets of modern computing. The foundation engages with policymakers and industry leaders to highlight the significance of open-source software in fostering innovation and driving technological advancements.

Furthermore, the Linux Foundation is instrumental in managing the governance of the Linux kernel. With the support of prominent maintainers and contributors, it provides a framework for decision-making and conflict resolution that values meritocracy and inclusivity. This governance model ensures that contributions are evaluated objectively based on their technical quality and alignment with the kernel's overarching goals, thereby upholding the integrity of the development process.

Security has emerged as a focal point in the Linux ecosystem, and the Linux Foundation has taken proactive steps to address it. By launching initiatives like the Core Infrastructure Initiative (CII), the foundation aims to improve the security of critical open-source projects, including the Linux kernel. This initiative seeks to provide resources, funding, and best practices to enhance the security posture of open-source software, recognizing that a secure kernel is vital for the reliability of countless systems across various domains.

The Linux Foundation's influence extends beyond the kernel itself, as it collaborates with other organizations, foundations, and consortiums to promote open-source innovation across various sectors, including cloud computing, IoT, networking, and artificial intelligence. Through these partnerships, the foundation helps shape the future of technology, ensuring that open-source principles remain central to the ongoing evolution of software development.

In summary, the Linux Foundation plays a crucial role in the development, governance, and promotion of the Linux kernel and the open-source community at large. Its efforts to foster collaboration, provide resources, and advocate for security and best practices have significantly contributed to the continued growth and relevance of Linux as a core operating system choice. As technology continues to evolve, the foundation's influence in shaping the future of Linux and the broader open-source ecosystem will remain essential in navigating challenges and driving innovation within the global digital landscape. Through a commitment to collaboration and shared goals, the Linux Foundation embodies the essence of what it means to be part of a vibrant open-source community, ultimately championing a future where technology is accessible, reliable, and secure for all.

6.2. Major Kernel Developers and Their Contributions

In the vast landscape of Linux kernel development, several major contributors have significantly shaped its evolution, each bringing unique skills, insights, and philosophies to the community. Understanding the contributions of these kernel developers provides invaluable context for recognizing the collaborative spirit that has driven the Linux kernel into a formidable force in the world of computing.

Linus Torvalds stands at the forefront as the creator of the Linux kernel, whose vision, advocacy for open-source principles, and unique leadership style have been fundamental to the kernel's success. Torvalds started the Linux project in 1991 as a personal endeavor to create a free operating system resembling Unix. However, what began as a hobby quickly transformed into a global phenomenon. His philosophy emphasized transparency, community engagement, and distributed collaboration, creating a welcoming environment for developers worldwide. Torvalds' hands-on approach to governance—periodically merging contributions while mentoring new developers—has been instrumental in fostering a collaborative culture focused on quality and meritocracy.

Beyond Torvalds, there are many other developers whose contributions have left a lasting impact on the kernel. One such figure is Andrew Morton, known for his work on the Linux kernel's memory management subsystem and as the maintainer of the -mm tree. The -mm tree serves as a staging area for new features, allowing developers to test potential changes before they are merged into the mainline kernel. Morton's efforts in debugging and reliability within the kernel have significantly improved the overall performance of Linux, providing a sandbox for experimentation that has led to many successful features.

Another crucial contributor is Greg Kroah-Hartman, recognized for his stewardship of the stable kernel tree and his role in driver development. As a prominent maintainer, Kroah-Hartman has advocated for more predictable and reliable releases, greatly enhancing the kernel's usability for end-users. His work on the USB subsystem has made it easier to plug and play devices on Linux, improving user experience. Furthermore, Kroah-Hartman's emphasis on clear communication and documentation has fostered a strong community around kernel development.

In the realm of security, numerous developers have pushed the boundaries of what is possible in kernel security. One such developer is James Morris, who has been pivotal in integrating Security-Enhanced Linux (SELinux) into the kernel. SELinux provides mandatory access control frameworks that enhance security by defining strict policies for system interactions. Morris's work has broadened awareness of security best practices in the Linux community, demonstrating the value of integrating robust security measures into operating system kernels.

The contributions of these developers extend to various subsystems; for example, David Miller has played a vital role in enhancing the networking stack. His commitment to optimizing network performance and protocol support through innovative contributions has established Linux as a robust choice for servers and networking devices. Miller's active engagement in the community has also fostered an inclusive dialogue around networking issues, promoting collaboration among a diverse group of developers.

Kernel developer Jessica Yu has been influential in introducing and advocating for the use of distributed development practices within the community. Her work on the module signing and auditing facilities has not only enhanced security but has also encouraged better practices around code reviews and vulnerability management among contributors. Yu's advocacy for diversity and inclusion in the kernel community has strengthened the foundation for future innovation and collaboration.

Anna Bon, known for her efforts in promoting accessibility within Linux, has also made significant strides in kernel contributions by designing features that cater to users with disabilities. Her approach highlights the need for inclusivity in open-source projects, encouraging other developers to consider diverse user experiences while contributing to the kernel.

The kernel's evolution has also been influenced by the collaborative efforts of organizations and companies that actively contribute developers to the community. Companies such as Red Hat, IBM, and Intel have established programs that incentivize their staff to engage with kernel development, ensuring that their contributions address both organizational interests and the broader needs of the Linux community.

In summary, the major kernel developers mentioned above, along with countless others, epitomize the essence of collaboration within the Linux community. Their contributions—ranging from technical improvements and code management to advocacy for security and inclusivity—have profoundly impacted the kernel's trajectory. Each developer, through their unique expertise and perspective, has woven a rich tapestry that reflects the values of openness, cooperation, and innovation at the heart of the Linux kernel. As the community continues to evolve, these contributions will guide and inspire future generations of developers and collaborators, ensuring that the Linux kernel remains a vibrant and integral part of the technology land-scape. In the collaborative spirit reminiscent of Linux's origins, every contribution matters, forging a future where technology flourishes through shared knowledge and a collective passion for progress.

6.3. Kernel Summits and Conferences

Kernel Summits and Conferences serve as vital conduits for collabo-ration, knowledge-sharing, and innovation within the Linux kernel community. These events bring together developers, contributors, and enthusiasts from diverse backgrounds to discuss advancements, challenges, and opportunities related to the Linux kernel. Under-standing the significance and impact of these gatherings is essential for grasping how the kernel continues to evolve in response to emerging technologies and user needs.

One of the most notable aspects of Kernel Summits and Conferences is their ability to foster face-to-face interactions among kernel developers. Through in-person discussions, participants can delve into intricate technical issues, propose solutions, and collaborate on projects that require collective brainstorming and expertise. These interactions often lead to new ideas and collaborations that might not have materialized in the virtual realm alone, capitalizing on the synergy of diverse perspectives and experiences.

The Linux Kernel Summit, held annually, serves as a key forum for discussing the high-level direction and management of the kernel project. This event gathers major maintainers, subsystem developers, and influential figures in the open-source world to engage in discussions that shape the future of the kernel. Topics addressed at these summits can range from resource management, architecture changes, and security enhancements to the governance model of the kernel itself. The discussions at these summits often result in actionable outcomes, driving the kernel's development trajectory and influencing project timelines.

In addition to the Kernel Summit, numerous other conferences dedicated to Linux and open-source software take place globally. Events like Linux Plumbers Conference and Linaro Connect focus on specific areas, such as plumbing within the Linux ecosystem and collaboration on embedded systems respectively. These events highlight specialized topics, allowing contributors to tackle particular challenges and share best practices that can significantly impact the kernel's development.

Throughout these conferences, workshops are held to facilitate hands-on learning and encourage developers to deepen their technical skill sets. Attendees can participate in sessions related to debugging techniques, performance optimization, and secure coding practices, enabling them to gain valuable insights that can be directly applied to their contributions. This educational aspect of conferences ensures that the Linux community remains at the forefront of technological advancements and that contributors are prepared to address current and future challenges.

Networking is another fundamental benefit of attending Kernel Summits and Conferences. Developers can meet face-to-face, build relationships, and collaborate with both well-established contributors and newcomers. These connections often lead to mentorship opportunities, collaboration on future projects, or partnerships that enhance kernel development. Moreover, as developers share their experiences, they contribute to building an inclusive and supportive community that fosters growth and learning, where every participant feels valued and empowered to contribute.

Sponsorship and support from organizations within the tech ecosystem are crucial for the success of these events. Major companies involved in Linux development often sponsor conferences to engage with their communities, showcase their contributions, and recruit new talent. These sponsors tend to host workshops, present keynotes, and participate in discussions, further enriching the experience for attendees. The presence of sponsors underscores the significance of the Linux kernel not only as an open-source project but also as a critical infrastructure component that supports numerous industries and technologies.

Online resources and communities also play a vital role in complementing the in-person interactions of conferences. After these events, summaries, presentations, and discussions are often made available through various online platforms, making it accessible for those who could not attend. This digital footprint ensures that the knowledge and insights generated during conferences reach a wider audience, fostering a global community of developers eager to engage with and contribute to the Linux kernel.

Furthermore, the evolution of virtual conferences has adapted to changing circumstances, enabling participation regardless of geographical barriers. This shift allows for increased inclusivity, where developers from underrepresented regions can participate in discussions and benefit from the wealth of knowledge shared by industry leaders. Virtual gatherings foster a global dialogue that can lead to impactful contributions and ideas representative of a diverse demographic.

The outcomes of Kernel Summits and Conferences extend far beyond the discussions held during these events. Many strategic decisions initiated at these conferences can ripple throughout the broader open-source community. The prioritization of new features, alterations to governance structures, and fundamental improvements in workflows often arise from the collective conversations occurring in these spaces. Consequently, understanding the importance of these gatherings reinforces the recognition that active participation in the kernel community is critical for shaping its future development trajectory.

In summary, Kernel Summits and Conferences represent a hallmark of the Linux kernel community, driving collaboration, innovation, and learning among developers. These events facilitate in-person interaction, knowledge sharing, and partnership building, ultimately shaping the future of the Linux kernel and its ecosystem. The importance of these gatherings lies not only in the discussions held but in the lasting relationships formed and the actionable outcomes that emerge from collective contributions. Through continued engagement in these summits and conferences, the Linux kernel community ensures that it remains vibrant, responsive to change, and equipped to tackle the challenges of tomorrow's technological landscape.

6.4. Online Forums and Resources

Online forums and resources are crucial pillars supporting the expansive landscape of Linux kernel development, creating avenues for collaboration, knowledge-sharing, and community engagement. These platforms enable developers, contributors, and users to communicate effectively, seek help, share expertise, and foster a sense of belonging within the Linux community. Understanding the various online forums and resources available is essential for anyone looking to engage with the kernel ecosystem, whether they are seasoned developers, beginners, or casual users.

One of the primary venues for discussion within the Linux kernel community is the multitude of mailing lists. These mailing lists serve as communication channels where contributors can pose questions, share patches, discuss bugs, and announce new features. The Linux kernel mailing list (LKML) is the central hub for all things related to the kernel, welcoming discussions on technical aspects, governance issues, and announcements from leading developers. Active participation in mailing lists allows contributors to engage directly with kernel maintainers and experienced developers, fostering a collaborative environment that drives the kernel's evolution.

Apart from mailing lists, discussion forums have emerged as valuable resources for community engagement and support. Websites such as Stack Overflow, LinuxQuestions.org, and the Ubuntu Forums allow users to seek assistance and share solutions concerning kernel-related inquiries. These platforms, utilizing question-and-answer formats, provide a wealth of knowledge compiled from the collective experiences of users across various distributions. While not dedicated solely to kernel development, these forums often feature kernel-related topics, allowing newcomers to learn from past discussions or share their own challenges.

The ever-growing landscape of social media has also influenced how contributors engage with one another. Platforms like Twitter, Reddit, and Discord have seen the formation of specialized groups focused on Linux kernel development. Subreddits such as r/linux and r/kernel allow users to share news, updates, and discussions about ongoing developments within the community. These platforms facilitate interactions where users can respond quickly to questions, share tips, and explore relevant articles or developments in kernel-related technologies.

Documentation is another invaluable resource for those diving into kernel development. The Linux kernel documentation project provides extensive, structured documentation that covers various aspects of kernel configuration, subsystem behavior, and coding guidelines. Documentation offers crucial insights into the kernel's architecture, helping developers understand how to navigate code, explore APIs, and follow best practices. Maintaining up-to-date, thorough documentation is a community responsibility that ensures smoother onboarding for new contributors.

In addition to official documentation, numerous online courses, tutorials, and guides on platforms like YouTube, Coursera, and specialized websites such as Linux Academy contribute to building knowledge within the community. These resources provide practical, hands-on instructions that guide developers through setting up development environments, writing modules, debugging techniques, and the finer aspects of kernel programming. They are especially beneficial for those who prefer visual or structured learning methods.

Webinars and online meetups have also become popular as a means to share insights and learn from industry experts. These events often feature presentations on important kernel topics, latest features, or upcoming releases, followed by interactive Q&A sessions. Organizations like the Linux Foundation frequently host such events, providing the community with opportunities to stay informed about specific kernel developments and trends.

The kernel community also benefits immensely from various open-source conferences where developers and users can convene to discuss relevant topics, deliver talks, and participate in workshops. Events like LinuxCon, the Linux Plumbers Conference, and Kernel Recipes provide invaluable platforms for knowledge exchange, collaboration, and networking among kernel developers. The insights and best practices shared during these conferences are vital for the community's ongoing growth and development.

Another essential component of the online resources available to kernel developers is the access to version control systems, specifically Git. Public repositories on platforms like GitHub and GitLab enable developers to explore the kernel's source code, delve into past revisions, and contribute their modifications. These sites facilitate discussions through comment threads and pull requests, ensuring that the collaborative spirit of open source continues to thrive.

Additional resources, such as security advisories, bug tracking systems, and specialized kernel development wikis, also significantly enhance the community's ability to engage effectively. Websites like Kernel Newbies provide a curated set of resources specifically aimed at new contributors, helping them navigate their entry into kernel development. Furthermore, tracking security vulnerabilities through platforms like the Open Source Vulnerability Database (OSV) and the Kernel CVEs system ensures that the community remains vigilant regarding threats that may arise.

In conclusion, online forums and resources form the backbone of the Linux kernel community, facilitating active engagement and collaborative development. From mailing lists and social media platforms to dedicated documentation and online courses, these resources create a rich environment where developers and users can connect, learn, and contribute meaningfully to the Linux kernel. As technology continues to evolve, the continued growth and evolution of these platforms will remain integral in fostering collaboration and ensuring that the Linux kernel retains its position as a leading force in open-source software development. Empowered by these resources, contributors will continue to come together, collectively advancing the kernel and shaping its future in the ever-changing landscape of technology.

6.5. Collaborations and Partnerships

In the dynamic landscape of software development, collaborations and partnerships emerge as fundamental components in the advancement of the Linux kernel. These alliances serve not only to enhance the quality and performance of the kernel but also foster communal knowledge-sharing, innovation, and resilience. Understanding the multifaceted nature of these collaborations, as well as the various forms of partnerships that guide kernel development, reveals essential strategies for continued success and growth within the ecosystem.

One of the most prominent aspects of collaboration within the Linux kernel community is the relationship between individual contributors and large organizations. Many leading technology companies, such as IBM, Google, and Red Hat, actively contribute to kernel development by employing skilled developers and providing resources to enhance the codebase. These companies often see the direct benefits of investing in kernel development, as they rely on Linux for their products, services, and infrastructure. Their involvement helps shape kernel features and optimizes performance, enabling faster feature deployment and broader hardware support.

The collaborative nature of these partnerships extends to sponsorship and funding initiatives. Through organizations like the Linux Foundation, companies can pool resources to support kernel development, sponsor events, and promote educational opportunities within the community. Such support facilitates the organization of conferences, workshops, and training programs, which in turn nurture the next generation of kernel developers and empower the community.

In addition to corporate partnerships, collaborations among independent developers and contributors play a critical role in expanding the community's knowledge base and enhancing the quality of the kernel. Peer reviews, the sharing of code snippets, and the exchange of ideas within mailing lists motivate developers to refine their contributions. This continued mutual support fosters a spirit of open collaboration, where the collective experience of contributors leads to innovative solutions and high-quality code.

Moreover, collaborative projects such as the Kernel CI (Continuous Integration) initiative exemplify how partnerships can drive kernel development towards greater performance and stability. By integrating testing frameworks that run automated tests on kernel changes, developers can quickly identify configuration issues, performance regressions, and bugs. This continuous feedback loop encourages developers to contribute patches with confidence, knowing they will be subjected to rigorous testing. Kernel CI embodies the synergy of collaborative efforts, as various participants—both individuals and organizations—come together to ensure the stability and reliability of the kernel.

Partnerships with research institutions and universities further enrich the kernel community's ecosystem. By engaging with academia, organizations gain access to cutting-edge research, fresh ideas, and emerging talent. Collaborative research projects often involve students and professors working alongside kernel developers on specific challenges or innovations. Such initiatives create opportunities for knowledge transfer and highlight the relevance of the kernel in various research fields, driving advancements in performance, security, and functionality.

The continual engagement within the kernel community highlights the necessity of open communication. Open-source projects thrive on transparency and inclusivity, and effective communication channels are vital for ensuring that contributions are harmonized. Mailing lists, forums, and social media channels serve as gathering points for discussions, aligning contributions toward shared goals.

Effective collaboration also embodies the importance of mentorship in kernel development. As experienced developers guide newcomers through the intricacies of kernel programming, they cultivate an environment conducive to growth and learning. This mentorship not only benefits individuals but also strengthens the community, as the transfer of knowledge accelerates innovation and fosters inclusivity.

Importantly, collaborations and partnerships in the Linux kernel extend to cross-project interactions as well. The Linux kernel interfaces with numerous other open-source projects, including userspace libraries and frameworks, which underscore the kernel's adaptability and relevance in various environments. The kernel community actively collaborates with developers from other projects, ensuring a harmonious interplay that drives the ecosystem forward.

In conjunction with these collaborative efforts, various partnerships with regulatory bodies, industry consortia, and open-source advocacy organizations help drive awareness and adoption of secure, high-performance software development practices within the kernel community. By participating in discussions around standards and security compliance, organizations and developers can align their efforts with the evolving expectations of the broader technology landscape.

Overall, collaborations and partnerships form the backbone of Linux kernel development, enabling seamless integration of diverse talents, experiences, and resources. These alliances promote mutual growth, innovation, and the crafting of a robust ecosystem where contributors from different backgrounds can thrive. By nurturing collaboration and forging strong partnerships, the Linux kernel community ensures its continuous evolution, sustaining its position at the forefront of open-source software development. Ultimately, the spirit of coopera-tion will continue to drive the kernel forward, empowering develop-ers and organizations alike to create pioneering solutions that shape the future of technology.

7. Performance Optimization

7.1. Analyzing Your System's Performance

Analyzing your system's performance in the context of the Linux kernel involves a multifaceted approach, combining various tools, methodologies, and frameworks to extract meaningful insights regarding how well your Linux system operates. Given the intricacies of modern computing environments, understanding performance characteristics can be pivotal for optimization, reliability, and efficient resource management.

The process begins by defining the performance metrics that matter for your specific use case. These metrics might include CPU utilization, memory consumption, disk I/O, network traffic, and response times for specific applications or services. Defining baseline performance targets is essential, as it provides clear objectives and allows for the measurement of improvements or degradations over time.

To get started on performance analysis, the first step is to utilize various monitoring tools available within the Linux ecosystem. Command-line utilities such as `top` and `htop` provide real-time insights into active processes and their resource usage. While `top` offers a basic view, `htop` enhances usability with its interactive interface, allowing users to sort and filter processes based on resource consumption. These tools enable administrators to quickly identify resource hogs or irregular behavior by overlapping statistical data with specific application performance.

For a deeper dive into performance metrics, tools such as `vmstat`, `iostat`, and `netstat` can be invaluable. With `vmstat`, users can monitor virtual memory statistics, providing key insights into how memory allocation, paging, and swapping affect system performance. Meanwhile, `iostat` offers detailed information regarding disk I/O, allowing administrators to gauge how efficiently storage devices are processing read and write requests. Similarly, `netstat` provides networking statistics, helping to assess traffic flow and diagnose potential bottlenecks in network communication.

System profiling can offer a nuanced view of how applications interact with the kernel and utilize system resources. Tools such as `perf` are specifically designed for performance profiling within Linux. By using `perf record`, developers can collect performance data during application execution, subsequently visualizing this data with `perf report`. Profiling allows users to identify hotspots—segments of code that consume excessive CPU cycles—enabling targeted optimizations to improve application efficiency.

When assessing system performance, it is also important to consider the kernel's scheduling and memory management mechanisms. Examining how the kernel allocates CPU time and manages memory can yield significant insights into system responsiveness and throughput. Memory descriptors and management frameworks such as `slab` and `slob` can influence how efficiently Linux handles allocations, affecting performance during heavy loads.

This awareness extends to kernel parameters that control the behavior of various subsystems. The `/proc/sys/` directory holds an array of tunable parameters that can be adjusted to enhance performance based on specific workloads. Parameters such as `vm.swappiness`, which controls the balance between swapping and caching, can have serious effects on memory performance and responsiveness. Administrators often employ tools like `sysctl` to make real-time adjustments to kernel parameters, allowing for rapid experimentation with resource allocation strategies.

In addition to dynamic analysis, capturing historical performance data is vital. The combination of utilities like `sar` (System Activity Reporter) enables users to log performance data over time, enabling trend analysis and historical comparisons. Alarms and alerts can also be set up by utilizing tools like `Nagios` and `Zabbix`, facilitating proactive monitoring to identify performance degradation before it affects system users.

Data visualization tools and dashboards, such as `Grafana` and `Kibana`, can further aid performance analysis by visualizing the metrics gathered from various monitoring tools. By presenting complex data in intuitive formats, these tools empower administrators to rapidly assess health and performance trends, making it easier to communicate findings with stakeholders or identify areas needing attention.

Collaboration is often essential in analyzing system performance. Engaging the Linux community via forums and mailing lists can enable discussions around common performance issues and solutions. Collaborating with others facing similar challenges fosters shared learning and grants access to diverse experiences that can enlighten individual analyses.

As the process of analyzing performance unfolds, it is essential to adopt a systematic methodology. This could involve starting with high-level observations, drilling down to specific areas of interest, implementing changes, and finally measuring the outcomes against the defined benchmarks. This cycle of analyzing, optimizing, and re-evaluating aligns with the principles of continuous improvement inherent in both software development and system administration.

In summary, analyzing your Linux system's performance involves a holistic approach that capitalizes on various tools, techniques, and community engagement. By combining dynamic monitoring with profiling, tuning kernel parameters, and historical data analysis, administrators can gain deep insights into system performance and implement effective strategies for optimization. The insights derived from performance analysis lay a foundation for ongoing improvements and reliability in the applications and services powered by the Linux kernel. Ultimately, a systematic approach to performance analysis not only enhances individual systems but fosters a culture of learning and collaboration within the Linux community, paving the way for sustained innovation.

7.2. Tuning the Kernel Parameters

Tuning the kernel parameters is a critical aspect of optimizing Linux system performance and behavior. The kernel, serving as the core interface between hardware and software, is governed by an array of parameters that define its operation regarding resource management, performance characteristics, and even security. By understanding how to effectively tune these parameters, system administrators and developers can tailor the Linux kernel to meet the specific needs of their environments, enhancing both efficiency and responsiveness.

First, it is important to identify the different classes of kernel parameters that can be tuned. These parameters can be broadly categorized into a few areas, including process scheduling, memory management, file system settings, network configuration, and system security. Each category contains a variety of specific kernel parameters that control different aspects of how the Linux system operates.

To access and modify these parameters, administrators can use the /proc/sys interface, which provides a virtual filesystem that allows for easy access to kernel parameters at runtime. Each parameter within this directory can be read and controlled, allowing administrators to both observe current settings and alter them as necessary. For instance, the value of vm.swappiness, which defines how aggressively the kernel swaps memory pages between RAM and disk, can be adjusted to optimize memory usage depending on workload requirements.

Modifying kernel parameters often requires administrative privilege; thus, many changes can be made using the sysctl command. This command provides a straightforward way to view and alter kernel parameters dynamically. For example, running sysctl vm.swappiness=10 will adjust the swappiness value to prioritize RAM usage, potentially improving performance in systems with ample memory resources. To make these changes persistent across reboots, users can modify the /etc/sysctl.conf file, adding entries for any parameters they wish to persist.

One commonly tuned parameter relates to process scheduling, particularly the variable kernel.sched_migration_cost_ns, which influences how quickly the scheduler can switch a running task to a different core. Administrators may adjust this value based on the architecture and workload of the system, potentially improving scheduling efficiency on multicore processors.

Memory parameters require careful consideration, particularly in environments with varied workloads. In addition to `vm.swappiness`, other relevant parameters include `vm.overcommit_memory`, which defines the kernel's behavior regarding memory allocation when physical memory is exhausted. This setting can be fine-tuned to prevent applications from overcommitting system resources indiscriminately.

Networking performance is another critical area where kernel parameters can be tuned. For instance, the `net.core.rmem_max` and `net.core.wmem_max` parameters control the maximum buffer sizes for receiving and transmitting data over network sockets. In environments with high network throughput, increasing these limits can lead to improved performance and reduced packet loss. Additionally, tuning the `tcp_max_syn_backlog` parameter controls the maximum number of queued connection requests that are pending acceptance, which can be particularly beneficial in handling spikes in traffic on a server.

Moreover, security parameters play a vital role in a well-tuned kernel, especially in production environments. Adjusting settings like `kernel.randomize_va_space`, which enhances Address Space Layout Randomization (ASLR), can significantly bolster the security posture of systems against certain types of attacks. Security-conscious administrators may also consider enabling certain kernel hardening features through the `/proc/sys/kernel` settings.

While tuning kernel parameters offers powerful capabilities to enhance performance and responsiveness, understanding the implications of these changes is equally essential. An untested change can have unforeseen consequences, leading to degraded performance or even system instability. Hence, it is wise to conduct thorough testing in a controlled environment prior to deploying changes in production systems. Monitoring system performance metrics before and after applying adjustments can provide valuable insights into the effectiveness of the tuning efforts.

Another approach to tuning involves leveraging automation and configuration management tools. Many DevOps practices encourage the usage of tools like Ansible, Puppet, or Chef to manage kernel parameter settings. This not only ensures consistency across multiple systems but also simplifies rollbacks in case undesirable effects emerge after changes.

In conclusion, tuning the kernel parameters represents a significant opportunity for system optimization, allowing practitioners to enhance performance, security, and responsiveness based on specific workload and usage patterns. Understanding the various kernel parameters accessible through the /proc/sys interface and utilizing tools like sysctl can empower system administrators and developers to fine-tune Linux systems effectively. Through diligent testing and monitoring, one can maximize system performance while maintaining stability and security, ultimately resulting in a more efficient computing environment tailored to meet diverse application needs. As users continue to engage in this critical practice, they not only enhance their systems but also contribute to the ongoing evolution and robustness of the Linux kernel as a whole.

7.3. Tools for Monitoring and Profiling

In the realm of modern computing, effective monitoring and profiling are indispensable practices for maintaining optimal system performance and reliability. Within the context of the Linux kernel, understanding the intricacies of these processes empowers developers and system administrators to proactively identify bottlenecks, diagnose issues, and refine system behavior. This subchapter delves into the diverse tools and techniques available for monitoring and profiling within the Linux environment, equipping readers with the knowledge to enhance system performance and address potential challenges.

Monitoring and profiling generally fall into distinct categories. Monitoring refers to the ongoing observation of system performance metrics, resource utilization, and overall system health. It offers real-time insights into how the system operates under various workloads and conditions. Profiling, on the other hand, involves analyzing the performance of specific code segments or subsystems to understand their behavior, resource consumption, and performance characteristics. Both practices are integral to optimizing kernel performance and ensuring system stability.

To begin monitoring, one of the fundamental tools at a user's disposal is the `top` command, which displays real-time information about active processes and their resource consumption. Users can ascertain CPU usage, memory allocation, and swap activity — essential indicators of system load and responsiveness. For more detailed insights, `htop` serves as a powerful alternative to `top`, offering an interactive interface that allows for sorting by various metrics and selecting specific processes for manipulation.

Another primary utility for monitoring resource usage is `vmstat`, which provides a wealth of information about memory, processes, CPU activity, and paging statistics. This command facilitates an understanding of how the system manages its memory and workload over time, enabling administrators to identify performance bottlenecks and optimize resource allocation.

Disk I/O is a critical component of performance, and tools such as `iostat` can help track input/output performance statistics for storage devices. By analyzing metrics like seek time and latency, users can pinpoint storage bottlenecks affecting overall system efficiency. Similarly, when monitoring network performance, the `netstat` tool provides essential insights into socket connections and protocol statistics, enabling effective network management and troubleshooting.

For more sophisticated performance monitoring, the `perf` tool holds a prominent place. It is invaluable for profiling kernel and application performance at a granular level. Users can leverage `perf record` to capture performance data while specific workloads are executing, then use `perf report` to display and visualize collected data. This profiling capability aids in identifying hotspots within the code or understanding where optimization efforts should be focused to enhance performance.

Beyond basic tools, the Linux kernel also offers more advanced monitoring features through `ftrace`, a powerful tracing utility that allows developers to track function calls, interruptions, and scheduling events. With `ftrace`, users can gather insights into how system functions perform relative to each other, providing invaluable data for diagnosing performance issues and making informed optimization decisions.

Moreover, kernel-based tracing applications, such as SystemTap and BPF (Berkeley Packet Filter), have gained popularity as they allow for dynamic instrumentation of the kernel. These tools enable developers to write scripts that monitor specific system behavior in real-time and efficiently gather performance data. BPF, in particular, has evolved significantly, now supporting a range of use cases beyond network filtering to include performance analysis, security, and observability.

As monitoring and profiling provide crucial insights into system performance, it is equally essential for users to share their findings and insights with the broader Linux kernel community. Engaging in discussions through mailing lists, forums, and conferences fosters a spirit of collaboration that drives continuous improvement in kernel performance and features.

Overall, the tools and techniques available for monitoring and profiling within the Linux kernel landscape are diverse and versatile. From interactive monitoring utilities like `top` and `htop` to sophisticated profiling capabilities via `perf`, `ftrace`, and dynamic tracing tools, developers have a robust toolkit to understand and optimize system performance effectively. This thorough analysis not only contributes to individual systems' efficiencies but also resonates within the larger Linux ecosystem, promoting an environment where continuous learning, collaboration, and innovation can flourish.

7.4. Best Practices for Optimization

In the complex landscape of Linux kernel development, optimization is paramount for ensuring that systems operate efficiently and effectively across diverse workloads. Best practices for optimization serve as guidelines that both seasoned developers and newcomers can follow to enhance kernel performance and application responsiveness. Understanding these practices enables developers to make informed decisions about system configuration, kernel parameters, and code contribution, ultimately leading to better-performing Linux systems.

To begin with, one of the key tenets of kernel optimization is to employ profiling and monitoring tools judiciously. Tools such as `perf`, `ftrace`, and `systemtap` allow developers to gather data about how the kernel and applications utilize system resources. Profiling involves examining which components of the kernel consume the most CPU, memory, and I/O bandwidth. This data provides crucial insights into specific areas that may benefit from optimization. For instance, by identifying functions that take up a substantial amount of CPU cycles, developers can focus on refining those functions to boost overall performance.

Another essential aspect of kernel optimization is to fine-tune kernel parameters based on the specific workload and hardware configuration. The `/proc/sys` interface provides a multitude of tunable parameters related to memory management, process scheduling, and networking. For example, adjusting `vm.swappiness` can influence how aggressively the kernel utilizes swap space, which is vital for memory-intensive applications. Similarly, fine-tuning network-related parameters—such as maximum TCP buffer sizes and the maximum number of queued connection requests—can enhance performance in network-heavy environments. It's important to test changes in a controlled environment to measure their impact and avoid introducing instability.

Effective memory management is crucial for optimization as well. The kernel employs various strategies to allocate and free memory, but examining memory usage patterns and avoiding fragmentation can significantly improve performance. Utilizing efficient memory allocation frameworks, like the slab allocator, can enhance the speed of memory operations. Developers should also be mindful of memory leaks and overhead associated with dynamic memory allocation, as these can lead to increased latency and resource exhaustion over time.

In addition, developers should practice good coding standards when contributing to the kernel. Clean, maintainable, and well-documented code is easier to optimize than poorly structured code. The Linux kernel coding style guide emphasizes consistency and readability, making the code more accessible to all contributors. Optimizing algorithms and data structures in the kernel can yield significant performance gains; therefore, developers should evaluate the complexity and efficiency of their solutions before submission.

Collaboration within the kernel community opens the door to shared knowledge and ideas regarding optimization techniques. Engaging in discussions on mailing lists, attending conferences, and participating in code reviews allow contributors to receive valuable feedback, identify potential pitfalls, and discover optimization strategies employed by others. The kernel community thrives on shared experiences, where collective problem-solving leads to innovative solutions and performance improvements.

Moreover, when optimizing, it is vital to maintain a balance between performance enhancements and code stability. Aggressive optimizations can inadvertently lead to bugs, security vulnerabilities, or reduced readability. Finding this balance often requires a willingness to iterate and assess trade-offs carefully. As each component of the kernel operates interdependently, ensuring that optimizations made in one area do not adversely impact others is critical for maintaining overall system integrity.

Utilizing automated testing and continuous integration systems, such as Kernel CI, can provide direct feedback on the impact of proposed changes. By integrating tests that evaluate both functionality and performance, developers can catch regressions early and ensure their optimizations have the desired effect without introducing instability.

Lastly, staying informed about the latest advancements and updates in Kernel development can help developers leverage new features or techniques that can simplify the optimization process. Adapting to changes in scheduling algorithms, memory management strategies, or new frameworks designed for performance can facilitate ongoing enhancements within the kernel.

In conclusion, best practices for optimization in the Linux kernel involve a combination of profiling, parameter tuning, efficient coding, collaboration, and testing. By employing these strategies mindfully, contributors can ensure their efforts lead to enhanced performance while maintaining the stability and integrity of the kernel. As the landscape of computing continues to evolve, embracing these best practices will empower developers to refine the Linux kernel and support the wide range of applications it encompasses. The pursuit of optimization is not just about performance gains; it's about crafting an operating system that remains robust, efficient, and accessible in a rapidly changing technological environment.

7.5. Common Pitfalls to Avoid

As you embark on your journey through the vast landscape of Linux kernel development, it's critical to recognize and steer clear of common pitfalls that can hinder progress and lead to frustration. These pitfalls, often encountered by newcomers and even seasoned contributors alike, can stem from misunderstandings of the kernel's architecture, poor coding practices, or ineffective collaboration. By arming yourself with knowledge of these pitfalls, you can navigate the kernel ecosystem more effectively and contribute with confidence.

One significant pitfall is underestimating the complexity of the Linux kernel. It is essential to appreciate that the kernel is a massive codebase with thousands of developers contributing across various subsystems. Newcomers may be tempted to dive headfirst into kernel development without a clear understanding of its intricacies. This approach can lead to missteps, such as proposing changes that conflict with existing functionality or submitting patches that fail to adhere to the kernel's coding guidelines. Before contributing, take the time to study the kernel's architecture, familiarize yourself with its subsystems, and read the extensive documentation available. Gaining a deeper understanding of the design principles and the underlying technologies will set you up for success.

Another common pitfall is neglecting the importance of testing. In the kernel development sphere, it is vital to thoroughly test your code changes before submission. Failing to do so can result in bugs or regressions affecting system stability and performance. It's crucial to implement robust unit tests, leverage automated testing frameworks, and engage with continuous integration systems such as Kernel CI to verify your changes under realistic scenarios. By emphasizing testing, you not only enhance the quality of your contributions but also build trust within the kernel community.

Effective communication is another area where pitfalls frequently arise. Kernel development thrives on collaboration, and clear communication is vital for success. When submitting patches, provide comprehensive commit messages that outline the purpose of your changes and the problem they address. Clarify your reasoning and highlight any relevant discussions from the mailing lists or elsewhere. Additionally, when engaging in code reviews or discussions, be open to feedback and recommendations. Remember that the kernel community values constructive dialogue and knowledge sharing, and remaining receptive to suggestions can strengthen your contributions.

A lack of patience can also lead to misfortune in kernel development. Contributions may not get immediate visibility or reception, leading to disillusionment or hasty decisions. The review process can often take time, with maintainers and reviewers managing a range of patches. It's essential to be respectful of this process and understand that quality takes precedence over speed. This patience will reward you with a deeper understanding of the community, allowing discussions to evolve naturally and fostering stronger relationships.

Diversification of knowledge within the kernel ecosystem is crucial, yet some developers may focus too narrowly on a specific area, leading to gaps in understanding. Kernel development spans numerous subsystems, and while stakeholders often specialize in particular areas, having a well-rounded knowledge base is beneficial. By exploring various subsystems and participating in discussions beyond your immediate expertise, you can approach problems more holistically and become a more valuable contributor.

Alongside these recommendations, be cautious of contributing excessively or prematurely to established subsystems without actively engaging with the respective maintainers. It is prudent to build rapport with maintainers for the subsystem you wish to contribute to, as they can provide insights, resources, and guidance on how best to align your contributions with community goals. Misalignment with the maintainers' direction can lead to wasted efforts or confusion regarding your intended contributions.

Lastly, be mindful of legacy code and accumulated technical debt within the kernel. While the kernel has evolved over decades, many areas of the codebase may be archaic or not align with modern best practices. Striking a balance between maintaining stability and cleaning up unrefined code can be challenging. When addressing legacy code, collaborate with others to approach improvements carefully, ensuring backward compatibility and thorough testing to avoid introducing new issues.

In summary, avoiding common pitfalls in Linux kernel development hinges on your understanding of the kernel's complexity, the importance of testing, effective communication, patience within the review process, diversification of knowledge, collaboration with maintainers, and careful handling of legacy code. As you navigate this intricate ecosystem, keep these lessons in mind, and you'll contribute more effectively while supporting the ongoing growth of the Linux kernel and its vibrant community. Embrace the rich history and collaborative spirit that the Linux kernel represents, and be ready to build upon it as you journey forward in your development endeavours.

8. The Art of Kernel Hacking

8.1. Kernel Hacking Essentials

Kernel hacking is a discipline that embodies the fusion of advanced technical skills and innovative problem-solving abilities, and it serves as a gateway to harnessing the true capabilities of the Linux kernel. To effectively engage in kernel hacking, one must be equipped with foundational knowledge, tools, and best practices that ensure productive contributions and optimizations to this complex, multifaceted system. This subchapter focuses on the essential elements that aspiring kernel hackers must grasp, laying the groundwork for successful exploration and modification of the Linux kernel.

To begin, it's vital to understand how the Linux kernel functions. The kernel operates as the core of the operating system, serving as the interface between hardware and software applications. It is responsible for resource management, process scheduling, memory allocation, and device management, among other critical functions. A sophisticated understanding of these components allows developers to navigate the interactions within the kernel and identify areas for improvement, optimization, or feature enhancement.

A fundamental aspect of kernel hacking is becoming familiar with the kernel source code. The Linux kernel is a continuously evolving codebase that is accessible to anyone interested in contributing. Developers can obtain the latest version of the kernel from repositories like kernel.org, where they can explore the source code, follow development discussions, and track changes over time. Thoroughly reading and understanding the code, particularly the areas related to your focus of interest, such as networking, file systems, or memory management, is essential for effective modification.

As you delve into the code, it's imperative to adopt clean coding practices and follow the Linux kernel coding style guidelines. This ensures that contributions align with the broader community's expectations, facilitating easier reviews and integration of your changes. The emphasis on clarity, consistency, and documentation is paramount;

ensuring that code is straightforward supports future maintainability and readability, ultimately fostering collaboration.

Another cornerstone of effective kernel hacking lies in mastering the art of debugging. Kernel development often presents unique challenges that require adept troubleshooting skills, particularly when dealing with complex issues that may lead to kernel panics or crashes. Familiarity with debugging tools such as gdb, kgdb, and ftrace enables developers to trace through kernel code, inspect variables, and analyze performance metrics while the kernel is running. Equipping oneself with these skills not only accelerates the debugging process but also enhances your ability to identify and resolve issues that arise during development.

Performance profiling serves as a critical extension of debugging, allowing kernel hackers to measure performance characteristics and resource usage. Tools like perf, systemtap, and oprofile provide insights into how system calls and kernel functions perform under various loads. By profiling specific components, developers can identify bottlenecks and inefficiencies, guiding optimizations that can lead to a more responsive and efficient system.

Collaboration within the Linux community reinforces the principles of kernel hacking. Engaging with fellow developers through mailing lists, forums, and code reviews generates opportunities for knowledge exchange. When submitting patches or discussing potential improvements, articulate your reasoning clearly and provide context for your changes. Thus, your contributions become integrated into the collective development process, enriching the shared expertise that drives kernel innovation forward.

A paramount consideration for kernel hacking is security, as the kernel operates at a privileged level and is vulnerable to various attack vectors. It's imperative to understand potential security concerns associated with your modifications. Adhere to secure coding practices, conduct thorough testing, and consider employing static analysis tools to identify vulnerabilities before submitting code. Emphasizing security not only protects the integrity of the kernel but also helps to foster trust within the community.

Kernel hacking also invites experimentation, allowing developers to try out new ideas and features. Creating custom kernel modules is a common practice, enabling the addition of functionality without altering the core kernel directly. By utilizing the kernel module framework, developers can write modules that interface with the kernel and extend its capabilities seamlessly. This modular approach facilitates easy loading and unloading of features while maintaining kernel stability.

As a kernel hacker, consider the broader implications of your work in the context of the Linux ecosystem. Understanding the ethical considerations of open-source development is essential, as contributors share a collective responsibility toward advancing features while maintaining quality and security. Participate in discussions around licensing, community norms, and collaborative practices to uphold the collaborative spirit synonymous with Linux kernel development.

In summary, kernel hacking is an essential skill set that combines a thorough understanding of the kernel's architecture, effective debugging strategies, performance profiling techniques, and community engagement. By prioritizing clean coding practices, security considerations, and collaboration, kernel developers can significantly enrich the Linux ecosystem. Embracing the challenges and rewards of kernel hacking cultivates a deeper appreciation for the power of open-source software, enabling individuals to make meaningful contributions that resonate across the technology landscape. As aspiring kernel hackers engage with this comprehensive toolkit, they embark on a compelling journey that elevates their skills, supports the development of the Linux kernel, and strengthens the collaborative community as a whole.

8.2. Dealing with Kernel Panics and Crashes

In the context of Linux kernels, dealing with kernel panics and crashes is one of the most critical aspects of maintaining system reliability and ensuring smooth operation. Kernel panics represent the kernel's last line of defense against catastrophic failures, where it encounters an unrecoverable error that necessitates halting operations to prevent data corruption or further damage. Understanding the mechanisms behind kernel panics, their causes, and the strategies for recovery and prevention is essential for developers and system administrators alike.

Kernel panics can be triggered by a variety of factors, including hardware malfunctions, memory corruption, improper configurations, or software bugs. One of the first steps in addressing a kernel panic is to examine the output generated by the kernel at the time of the panic. The panic message often provides clues regarding the specific error that occurred and can guide troubleshooting efforts. Typical symptoms of a kernel panic may include a frozen screen, a log message about a failed operation, or a stack trace indicating where the failure originated.

To effectively deal with kernel panics, it is beneficial to enable kernel debugging features. This can involve compiling the kernel with debugging options, which allows for capturing more detailed information regarding kernel operations and system state when a panic occurs. Enabling features like the "Kernel Crash Dumps" functionality is crucial in this context. This capability ensures that, upon panicking, the system saves a snapshot of the kernel memory to a persistent location, allowing developers to analyze the state of the system after the fact.

When a panic occurs, the kernel captures a core dump that can be analyzed to find the root cause of the issue. Using tools like "kdump," developers can configure systems to create core dumps automatically. Once collected, kernel debugging tools such as "crash" can be employed to review the core dump and examine the state of the kernel at the moment of failure. By analyzing the stack trace and memory contents, developers can pinpoint the offending code or operation, facilitating a deeper understanding of what led to the panic.

Besides addressing immediate concerns, preventing kernel panics begins with a proactive approach to system configuration and management. Ensuring that all hardware components are compatible with the Linux kernel and are running the latest firmware can significantly reduce the likelihood of hardware-induced panics. Moreover, stress testing the system under various workloads can help identify stability issues before they manifest in production settings. Regularly updating the Linux kernel to the latest stable version can also help, as newer releases often introduce bug fixes and enhancements that rectify known causes of crashes.

Monitoring system logs is equally important in combating kernel panics. System logs, often managed by tools like "syslog," "journalctl," or "dmesg," contain valuable information regarding events leading up to a crash, allowing for an analysis of recurring issues or conditions that instigate panics. By routinely reviewing these logs, administrators can catch warning signs before they escalate into catastrophic failures.

In response to frequent kernel panics, developers may need to engage in code review and testing before submitting substantial changes to the kernel. Code reviews within the kernel community help ensure that contributions align with established best practices and have been thoroughly vetted for potential issues. Implementing continuous integration tools that automatically test new changes against a suite of existing use cases is also crucial for catching issues proactively.

When it comes to addressing kernel crashes related to specific processes or features, employing kernel parameters and boot options can mitigate risks. Parameters such as `panic`, which specifies how long the kernel should wait before rebooting after a sudden crash, can be adjusted to provide sufficient time for developers to capture crucial information about the panic. Additionally, kernel boot options allow administrators to specify flags that affect kernel behavior during startup, enabling troubleshooting for particular drivers or behaviors in isolated modes.

It is also important to have a recovery plan in place for situations that lead to kernel panics. Configuring systems with redundant components, failover strategies, and regular backups can help ensure that data is not lost and that users can quickly restore services in the event of a panic.

In summary, dealing with kernel panics and crashes in Linux requires a balanced approach of reactive and proactive strategies. Understanding the causes, enabling appropriate debugging features, capturing kernel dump data, and engaging in diligent system monitoring are critical components in managing kernel stability. By implementing best practices for kernel development, rigorous testing, and system configuration, administrators can reduce the risk and impact of kernel panics, ensuring their systems remain reliable and resilient. Effectively navigating the complexities of kernel crashes forms a vital part of maintaining Linux systems, safeguarding data while supporting the collective innovation that the Linux community epitomizes.

8.3. Noise in Code: Cleaning Up Legacy Code

In the lifespan of any software project, especially one as complex and dynamic as the Linux kernel, the passage of time inevitably leads to the accumulation of legacy code. This is often manifested as outdated practices, obsolete functions, and suboptimal algorithms that no longer meet the needs of modern computing environments. As developers undertake the crucial task of maintaining the kernel's efficacy, cleaning up this legacy code becomes paramount. This process not only enhances performance and security but also benefits the overall community by fostering clarity and ease of contribution.

Assessment is the first crucial step in cleaning up legacy code. It requires a comprehensive review of the existing codebase to identify problematic areas. Tools such as `grep`, `find`, and static analysis tools can be immensely helpful for this. They can assist in locating deprecated functions, unused variables, and areas where memory management practices have fallen short of current standards. From this evaluation, developers can prioritize elements of the code that require immediate attention, based on their impact on system performance, maintainability, and overall security.

A critical aspect of this assessment involves understanding the legacy context. Code might have been written under specific constraints or philosophies that were not fully articulated or documented. As such, the motivations behind certain implementation choices should be explored to avoid the accidental removal of functionality relied upon by existing users or subsystems. Engaging with the community through mailing lists or forums can provide valuable insights into historical decisions, streamlining the cleanup process while maintaining alignment with the kernel's overarching objectives.

Once identified, the elimination or refactoring of legacy code should be approached with careful consideration for backward compatibility. Developers are often challenged to reconcile the urge to modernize with the need to uphold existing functionality for users who may still depend on legacy features. This can be achieved through gradual transitions, such as implementing updates in phases. For instance, deprecated functions might be flagged as such, providing warning messages while keeping them operational for a period. During this time, documentation can be updated, advocacy campaigns can be launched to encourage users to shift toward new alternatives, and eventually, the code can be safely removed.

Contributors should also be aware of the coding practices that align with contemporary kernel architecture. Following the established style guidelines improves readability and aids in future maintenance. Leveraging modern APIs, frameworks, or subsystems can offer improvements over legacy implementations. For instance, moving from older memory allocation techniques to new APIs that utilize more efficient data structures can lead to better performance and reliability.

Documentation plays a critical role in this cleanup effort as well. As code is refined or rendered obsolete, it's essential to update associated documentation accordingly. Comprehensive documentation enhances understanding and usability, allowing future contributors to grasp the current architecture and rationale for decisions made. Equally important is the creation of a clear transition plan for any end-users. Whether through changelogs or update notes, transparency regarding modifications helps the community acclimatize to changes, fostering goodwill and collaboration.

Testing is a non-negotiable element in the cleanup process. The kernel's integration tests, coupled with unit tests specific to the areas being refactored, should be executed rigorously to ensure that legacy function removal or modifications do not inadvertently introduce regressions or new issues. Automated testing frameworks can streamline this process, ensuring that system behavior remains consistent as the kernel's codebase evolves.

As developers undertake the task of cleaning up legacy code, open communication with the kernel community remains instrumental. Engaging maintainers, soliciting feedback, and participating in discussions can enrich one's understanding of the broader context in which the work exists. Furthermore, sharing experiences and the outcomes of cleanup efforts can inform and inspire the community, encouraging collaborative actions aimed at improving the kernel.

Finally, cleaning up legacy code is not merely an operational challenge; it embodies the ethos of the Linux community—a commitment to continuous improvement, transparency, and collaboration. Developers are encouraged to view this process as an ongoing effort rather than a one-time task. As the computing landscape evolves, so too must the code that powers Linux. By actively engaging in the cleanup process, contributors help to create a more robust, secure, and efficient kernel that reflects and responds to the needs and expectations of its user base—an endeavor that honors both the past and the future of this remarkable open-source project.

8.4. Creating Custom Kernel Modules

Creating custom kernel modules represents a pivotal aspect of kernel hacking, as it allows developers to extend the Linux kernel's functionality without the need for recompilation of the entire kernel. This flexibility not only enhances the adaptability of the Linux system but also provides a powerful means to integrate new features, drivers, or subsystems tailored to specific hardware or application requirements. Understanding the process of creating and managing custom kernel modules is essential for anyone aspiring to leverage the full capabilities of the Linux kernel in their projects.

To embark on the journey of creating custom kernel modules, developers must first establish a suitable development environment. This involves installing necessary tools and header files corresponding to the version of the kernel that is currently running. A typical toolchain for kernel module development includes `gcc` (the GNU Compiler Collection), `make` (a build automation tool), and appropriate kernel headers, which can usually be installed through the package management system of the Linux distribution in use.

The fundamental building block for writing a kernel module is the module source file, often written in C. A simple kernel module typically requires a minimum of two essential functions: `module_init()` and `module_exit()`. The `module_init()` function serves as the entry point for the module upon loading it into the kernel, executing the code necessary for initialization. In contrast, the `module_exit()` function is called when the module is removed from the kernel, facilitating cleanup operations such as freeing allocated resources or unregistering functionalities.

To load a kernel module, developers utilize the `insmod` command, which inserts the compiled module file (with a `.ko` extension) into the running kernel. Conversely, the `rmmod` command removes the module, invoking the cleanup routines implemented in the `module_exit()` function. Effective use of these commands allows for quick testing and iteration during the development process.

As custom modules interact closely with the kernel, it's essential to be diligent about error handling and resource management. Considerations must be made to handle the successful allocation of memory and any possible errors during initialization, as an improperly functioning module can lead to system crashes or instability.

Providing detailed logging within kernel modules is also a beneficial practice. The `printk()` function, analogous to `printf()` in user-space programming, can be employed for outputting messages to the kernel log. Different log levels, such as `KERN_INFO` or `KERN_ERR`, allow developers to categorize messages, facilitating easier debugging and monitoring during the module's operation.

A critical aspect of kernel module development is adherence to the kernel's coding standards and guidelines. Following the kernel coding style, including naming conventions, whitespace usage, and proper commenting practices, enhances code maintainability and promotes better collaboration with other developers. This attention to detail reflects respect for the community's norms and ensures that contributions can be smoothly integrated into the broader kernel ecosystem.

When implementing specific functionalities within custom kernel modules, developers can take advantage of various kernel APIs that facilitate interaction with kernel subsystems. This might include working with device drivers, file systems, or networking stacks. APIs offer valuable abstractions that simplify complex operations, allowing developers to focus on their specific objectives rather than managing low-level details.

Testing kernel modules is imperative, particularly in capturing the behavior of the module in various conditions. Unit tests can be devised to assess individual functionalities and confirm their efficiency independent of other components. Additionally, rigorous integration testing should take place to ensure that modules can coexist without adverse interactions.

Another consideration is the need for strong security practices when developing custom kernel modules. Modules operate at a high privilege level, making them susceptible to vulnerabilities that can compromise the entire system. Developers must follow secure coding practices to prevent issues like buffer overflows and validate inputs rigorously. Employing kernel debugging tools and dynamic tracing can also help identify vulnerabilities at runtime.

In exploiting the modularity of the Linux kernel, developers should consider the implications of kernel module dependencies. If a custom module relies on another module or subsystem, it is essential to ensure that all dependencies are present and properly loaded. Managing these relationships can prevent system errors and conflicts, enhancing the smooth operation of configured modules.

In summary, creating custom kernel modules provides an imperative pathway for extending the capabilities of the Linux kernel while embracing its open-source ethos. By mastering module development —understanding initialization and cleanup routines, employing robust logging, adhering to coding standards, testing comprehensively, and considering security implications—developers can effectively contribute to the Linux ecosystem. As the kernel continues to evolve, the creation of custom modules will remain a powerful tool in shaping tailored solutions to meet diverse technological challenges, fostering innovation and enhancing system capabilities across various domains.

8.5. Security Concerns in Kernel Code

In the context of kernel development, security concerns in kernel code are paramount due to the kernel's role as the core of the operating system, managing resources and facilitating communication between hardware and software. Security vulnerabilities within the kernel can lead to significant risks, including system crashes, data breaches, and unauthorized access to sensitive information. As such, developers must approach kernel code with a security-first mindset, implementing best practices and leveraging available tools to mitigate risks.

One of the most glaring security concerns in kernel code arises from the fact that the kernel operates at a high privilege level. This elevated access means that any flaws or vulnerabilities can lead to severe consequences, enabling attackers to execute arbitrary code, escalate privileges, or gain access to protected resources. Consequently, all code must be scrutinized meticulously to identify potential weaknesses.

Buffer overflows are a common vulnerability in C-based code, including kernel modules. These occur when a program writes more data to a buffer than it can hold, leading to memory corruption and potential execution of malicious code. Developers can mitigate this risk by following safe coding practices, such as using functions that enforce buffer limits (e.g., `strncpy` instead of `strcpy`) and conducting thorough input validation throughout the code.

Another area of concern is proper memory management. Kernel developers must be wary of memory leaks and double frees, which can lead to instability and potentially provide attack vectors for malicious users. Tools like `kmemleak` and `slabdebug` can help detect memory-related issues, enabling developers to identify and rectify them before they introduce vulnerabilities in production.

Race conditions pose another critical security risk, particularly in concurrent environments where multiple processes access shared resources. Exploiting a race condition may allow an attacker to manipulate the behavior of a process, leading to unauthorized access or privilege escalation. To mitigate race conditions, developers should employ proper synchronization mechanisms, such as mutexes and semaphores, ensuring that critical sections of code are protected from concurrent modifications.

Additionally, user input validation cannot be overlooked when developing kernel code. Proper validation ensures that inputs do not lead to unexpected behavior or vulnerabilities. Developers should enforce strict checks on parameters passed to kernel functions, ensuring that inputs conform to expected types, ranges, and formats.

In the realm of kernel security, the use of security modules is essential. The Linux kernel offers several security frameworks, such as SELinux (Security-Enhanced Linux) and AppArmor, that enable fine-grained access control and policy enforcement. Integrating these security modules into kernel code can help developers enforce strict access controls and minimize the impact of potential vulnerabilities.

Furthermore, ensuring kernel code integrity is crucial for maintaining a secure environment. Developers can leverage cryptographic techniques, such as signing kernel modules, to verify their authenticity before loading them into memory. This practice helps to prevent the execution of tampered or unauthorized code that could jeopardize system security.

Another vital aspect of security in kernel code is the timely application of patches and updates. The Linux community actively tracks vulnerabilities and issues, releasing patches to address them. Staying current with these updates is essential to ensure that systems remain protected against known vulnerabilities. Organizations that utilize Linux may consider implementing automated systems or proper policies to manage and apply kernel updates seamlessly.

It is important for developers to conduct regular audits of kernel code to identify potential vulnerabilities and gaps in security. Peer reviews and collaborative code evaluation processes within the community facilitate this practice, encouraging developers to share knowledge and conduct thorough examinations of each other's contributions.

Effective documentation is also a key element in maintaining security within kernel code. Clear and comprehensive documentation allows developers to understand the rationale behind design decisions, security practices, and functions necessary for proper maintenance. This practice contributes to a shared understanding of security concerns and helps prevent misunderstandings that may lead to vulnerabilities being introduced inadvertently.

Lastly, security training and awareness programs are vital to fostering a security-conscious culture among kernel developers. Providing resources and education on secure coding practices, threat modeling, and vulnerability assessment empowers developers to recognize potential risks in their code and equips them with the knowledge to mitigate those risks proactively.

In conclusion, security concerns in kernel code demand rigorous attention from developers due to the kernel's critical role in system integrity and resource management. By adhering to best practices, leveraging security frameworks, effectively managing memory, conducting regular audits, and prioritizing timely updates, developers can significantly enhance the security of kernel code. As the Linux kernel continues to evolve, fostering a proactive security culture within the community is vital to mitigate risks and ensure the robustness of the kernel and the systems it powers. The collective responsibility of kernel developers to engage in secure practices ultimately strengthens the entire Linux ecosystem and contributes to the trust users place in the technology.

9. Real-time Kernel and Embedded Systems

9.1. Understanding Real-time Expectations

In the realm of modern computing, the demand for real-time capabilities is increasing, influencing numerous domains, from telecommunications to automotive systems and beyond. Understanding real-time expectations is crucial for developers, engineers, and system architects working in environments that require strict timing constraints. In the context of the Linux kernel, real-time systems must operate with predictability and determinism, ensuring that time-sensitive tasks are executed within specified time limits. This subchapter examines the factors contributing to real-time expectations and how developers can leverage the Linux kernel to meet these requirements successfully.

Real-time systems fall into two main categories: hard real-time and soft real-time systems. Hard real-time systems have stringent requirements, where missing a deadline could result in catastrophic failures, such as in medical devices or safety-critical applications in aviation. Conversely, soft real-time systems can tolerate occasional deadline misses, although systematic delays can significantly affect overall performance, as seen in multimedia streaming and online gaming. Understanding the distinction between these types sets the foundation for tailoring kernel features to meet the specific challenges associated with real-time applications.

Linux, by default, is designed for general-purpose computing and may not fulfill the exact real-time requirements without further modification. However, the kernel has incorporated features that can be leveraged to enhance real-time performance. One of the key attributes of a real-time system is the ability to manage task scheduling effectively. In a real-time context, the scheduler must prioritize critical tasks, guaranteeing that they receive the necessary CPU time to complete their operations promptly. The Completely Fair Scheduler (CFS), employed by default in many Linux systems, aims for fairness among tasks but may not suffice for strict real-time needs.

To address real-time expectations, the Linux kernel offers the option to utilize the PREEMPT-RT patch, which transforms the kernel into a preemptive real-time operating system. This patch enhances the task scheduling capabilities, allowing high-priority tasks to interrupt lower-priority ones. The PREEMPT-RT patch also introduces a range of kernel modifications to reduce latencies, making it an invaluable tool for developers working on real-time applications. Understanding how to configure and implement this patch plays a pivotal role in aligning Linux with real-time performance needs.

Moreover, understanding interrupt handling is critical for real-time responsiveness. A real-time kernel must minimize interrupt latency, ensuring that time-sensitive tasks can be executed as quickly as possible following an interrupt. Developers should familiarize themselves with interrupt handling mechanisms and leverage techniques such as interrupt affinity—binding specific interrupts to dedicated CPU cores —to achieve consistent latency behavior. Additionally, judicious use of locking mechanisms and reducing contention in critical sections can further enhance the kernel's real-time capabilities.

Real-time expectations extend to memory management as well. Memory allocation techniques, such as the use of real-time allocators and low-latency memory management strategies, are imperative in maintaining performance under real-time constraints. For instance, a specialized memory allocation framework designed for real-time systems can be employed to minimize overhead and fragmentation, allowing the kernel to access memory without introducing unpredictable latencies.

Another essential aspect of real-time systems is the management of system resources, including CPU frequency scaling and power management. Operating systems must balance performance with energy efficiency, particularly in embedded systems and IoT devices. Understanding how to configure CPU governors can significantly impact system responsiveness in real-time applications, providing the agility required to meet varying workloads.

Testing and validation in real-time environments are also critical. Developers should conduct rigorous testing to ensure that the system meets its timing requirements under scenarios that mimic actual operating conditions. Tools designed for benchmarking and profiling real-time systems—such as cyclictest and latencytop—help measure latencies, inform tuning decisions, and highlight areas for performance improvements.

Importantly, collaboration plays a role in aligning expectations with real-world constraints. Engaging with the Linux kernel community through mailing lists, forums, and conferences is invaluable for gathering insights, sharing experiences, and learning from other developers who have tackled similar real-time challenges. As the landscape of real-time applications evolves, staying informed about the latest developments and best practices can enhance the effectiveness of real-time Linux systems.

In conclusion, understanding real-time expectations is vital for developing systems that require strict timing constraints and predictability. By leveraging features such as the PREEMPT-RT patch, optimizing interrupt and memory handling, and engaging with the kernel community, developers can tailor the Linux kernel to align with real-time requirements. As technology continues to evolve, distilling real-time practices from the kernel community will pave the way for innovation in applications where time is of the essence. Through a commitment to real-time readiness, developers can empower their systems to thrive in dynamic, real-world environments, delivering crucial functionality in the fast-paced digital landscape.

9.2. Implementing Real-time Features

The implementation of real-time features within the Linux kernel hinges upon understanding the principles and methodologies that facilitate timely and predictable system behavior. Real-time computing asserts that certain tasks must be completed within strict time constraints, where failures to meet those constraints can result in system failures or undesired operations. Consequently, tailoring the Linux kernel to serve real-time applications necessitates a multifaceted approach, encompassing kernel configuration, scheduling methodologies, and development practices specifically designed for efficiency and responsiveness.

At the heart of implementing real-time features is the necessity to select an appropriate scheduling algorithm. In standard Linux distributions, the Completely Fair Scheduler (CFS) pertains to a general-purpose model that may lack the predictability required for real-time tasks. To achieve real-time performance, developers often utilize the PREEMPT-RT patch, a modification that enhances the kernel's ability to preempt tasks that are currently being executed. This patch works by ensuring that high-priority tasks can interrupt lower-priority ones, minimizing the latencies associated with task switching. Implementing this patch necessitates thorough testing to ensure it fulfills the specific latency requirements dictated by real-time applications.

In addition to the CFS modifications provided by the PREEMPT-RT patch, the priority of tasks must be managed meticulously. The Linux kernel allows the assignment of static real-time priorities to tasks, offering Priority Inheritance and FIFO (First In, First Out) scheduling policies that can be particularly valuable in real-time environments. Developers must be mindful when assigning these priorities, as improper configurations can lead to priority inversion—a scenario where lower-priority tasks preempt higher-priority ones, disrupting the intended execution flow.

Memory management also plays a critical role in optimizing real-time features. The kernel must allocate and deallocate memory with minimal latency, as unpredictable memory access can hinder time-sensitive operations. Developers can utilize slab allocators or specialized memory pools optimized for real-time applications to achieve predictable memory access patterns. Moreover, ensuring that memory resources are allocated proactively—rather than reactively—enables systems to achieve the requisite performance levels under various workloads.

To manage I/O operations effectively, it is essential to consider the implications of I/O scheduling on real-time features. Reverting to the Completely Fair Queueing (CFQ) I/O scheduler may lead to undesirable latencies encountered in traditional block devices. Rather, developers can opt for I/O schedulers designed for responsiveness, such as the Deadline or Noop schedulers, which can prioritize tasks based on predefined time constraints, thereby ensuring that time-sensitive data is processed without undue delay.

As developers work towards implementing real-time features, they should also adopt best practices in code quality and optimization. Efficient code structure, effective error handling, and a focus on low-latency operations are paramount. Adopting coding conventions aligned with kernel practices facilitates collaboration and maintainability. Rigorous testing of kernel modifications should be prioritized, ensuring all components work cohesively under real-time demands.

Moreover, debugging and profiling tools tailored for real-time systems allow developers to monitor system behavior, analyze task latencies, and troubleshoot issues effectively. Tools such as `latencytop`, `cyclictest`, and `perf` can identify prevalent bottlenecks, leading to further optimizations. Utilizing these tools enables developers to pinpoint areas where changes may be necessary and assess the overall impact of their optimizations on real-time performance.

Engagement with the kernel community is crucial for sharing insights and experiences regarding real-time implementations. Collaborations via mailing lists or forums pave the way for discussions that can refine approaches to common challenges, facilitate sharing of effective strategies, and foster a collective knowledge base that enhances the overall effectiveness of real-time Linux products.

In conclusion, implementing real-time features within the Linux kernel demands a robust understanding of scheduling strategies, memory management, I/O operations, and code quality practices. Tailoring the kernel to meet precise timing requirements equips developers to create applications capable of performing under the stringent constraints of real-time computing. By leveraging the tools and resources available within the Linux community, as well as employing thorough testing and profiling methodologies, developers can build robust; responsive systems that thrive in real-time environments. Ultimately, these efforts reinforce the Linux kernel's adaptability, pushing the boundaries of modern computing wherever precision and reliability are paramount.

9.3. The Role of Linux in IoT

In the rapidly advancing landscape of technology, the Internet of Things (IoT) has emerged as a transformative force, connecting a multitude of devices to the internet and enabling unprecedented levels of interconnectivity, automation, and data exchange. At the heart of this burgeoning ecosystem lies the Linux operating system, which has established itself as a foundational platform for the development and deployment of IoT devices. Its open-source nature, flexibility, and robustness make Linux ideally suited for the diverse needs of IoT applications spanning various industries, from smart home devices to industrial automation. This section delves into the fundamental role Linux plays in the IoT space, examining its advantages, the challenges it faces, and its potential for future evolution.

One of the most significant advantages of Linux in the IoT realm is its adaptability. The kernel can be customized to fit the specific constraints of myriad IoT devices, which can range from powerful servers to resource-constrained microcontrollers. Many lightweight distributions of Linux, such as Yocto, Buildroot, and Alpine Linux, have been developed specifically for embedded environments, providing developers with the tools to create tailored operating systems that run efficiently on limited resources. This versatility has resulted in the ability to deploy Linux across an extensive variety of devices, from single-board computers like Raspberry Pi to industrial sensors and gateways.

Furthermore, the extensive ecosystem of drivers and modularity of the Linux kernel give developers access to an abundance of hardware options. As new IoT devices enter the market, manufacturers have the opportunity to leverage existing Linux drivers or create new modules that facilitate communication with varied sensors and actuators. This interconnectedness ensures that developers can integrate diverse components into their IoT projects without starting from scratch, thus accelerating the development process.

Security is a paramount concern within the IoT landscape due to the vast quantities of sensitive data being collected and transmitted among devices. The inherent design of the Linux kernel, along with its active development community, allows for robust security features to be implemented and updated regularly. Security enhancements, such as mandatory access controls through SELinux or AppArmor, alongside effective patch management practices, empower developers to build secure IoT systems. Additionally, the open-source nature of Linux enables rapid responses to newly discovered vulnerabilities, ensuring that IoT devices remain secure against potential threats.

Given the global and diverse nature of the IoT space, collaboration among developers is essential. The Linux community fosters a vibrant ecosystem that encourages knowledge sharing and collaboration through extensive documentation, forums, and conferences. Developers can access a wealth of resources, including project-specific information, best practices, and emerging technologies, all designed to aid in the successful deployment of their IoT solutions. The spirit of open-source collaboration ensures that anyone can contribute, fostering an inclusive environment where innovation thrives.

Despite the myriad advantages of using Linux in IoT, several challenges persist. One of the critical issues is the fragmentation of the IoT landscape. With numerous device types, operating environments, and use cases, developers may face inconsistencies in implementation and compatibility. This fragmentation necessitates that Linux adapt to various hardware, protocols, and ecosystems, which can complicate development efforts and create interoperability concerns.

Resource constraints can also pose challenges when deploying Linux on IoT devices. While the kernel is highly adaptable, developers must ensure that their customized versions remain lightweight and efficient. This sometimes necessitates trade-offs between features and resource utilization, making it essential that developers optimize their systems for performance without compromising functionality.

Additionally, as the number of devices connecting to the internet grows, concerns surrounding security and privacy continue to mount. The need for secure communication protocols, user privacy safeguards, and data protection mechanisms must be integral to any Linux-based IoT solution. Developers must remain vigilant, implementing best practices in security while considering the broader implications of their contributions on user trust and data integrity.

Looking ahead, the role of Linux in IoT is poised to expand further. The rise of edge computing, where processing occurs closer to the source of data generation, presents new possibilities for Linux deployments, enabling rapid response times and smarter processing in real-time applications. Additionally, technological advancements in artificial intelligence (AI) and machine learning (ML) can be seamlessly integrated into Linux-based IoT solutions, facilitating more intelligent automation, predictive maintenance, and smarter decision-making processes.

In conclusion, the role of Linux in the Internet of Things underscores its significance as a versatile, adaptable, and secure platform for developing IoT systems. With the ability to customize the kernel for diverse environments, leverage collaboration within the open-source community, and enhance security protocols, Linux stands as a critical foundation for the future of interconnected devices. As challenges persist, the continued evolution of Linux will be essential in shaping a more responsive, secure, and innovative IoT landscape, reinforcing its importance as a backbone for modern technological advancement.

9.4. Challenges in Embedded Linux Systems

In the landscape of technology, embedded Linux systems are becoming increasingly ubiquitous, powering a variety of devices from consumer electronics to critical industrial machinery and autonomous vehicles. However, the journey to successfully deploy embedded Linux systems is riddled with challenges that developers and engineers must navigate. Recognizing these challenges provides crucial insights for establishing robust and reliable embedded systems while leveraging the full potential of Linux.

One significant challenge in embedded Linux systems is resource limitation. Unlike traditional computing environments, embedded devices often come with constraints in processing power, memory, and storage capacity. These limitations demand careful consideration regarding the selection of kernel features and the implementation of software solutions. Developers must optimize their applications to ensure they run efficiently within these constraints, making choices that balance functionality with resource utilization. A common strategy involves building a minimal Linux distribution tailored specifically for the target hardware, stripping down unnecessary components and services to maximize performance.

Real-time requirements present another hurdle in embedded Linux systems, particularly in applications that demand precise timing and predictability. For instance, in automotive systems, timely responses to immediate stimuli are critical for safety and performance. Standard Linux kernels may lack real-time capabilities; therefore, developers often turn to alternatives like the PREEMPT-RT patch, which enhances timestamp precision and task scheduling. Implementing real-time features involves additional complexities, as developers must understand how to prioritize tasks effectively and minimize interruptions while still ensuring predictable behavior.

Compatibility with hardware is another challenge often faced in embedded Linux systems. As the diversity of devices grows, the need for supporting various architectures and peripherals becomes pivotal. Developers must ensure that their chosen kernel version has adequate driver support for the specific hardware components employed. Sometimes, this requires writing custom drivers, which can be a daunting task if thorough knowledge of the kernel's architecture and driver model is not achieved. Carefully researching existing drivers and engaging with the community can mitigate development risks while ensuring that the system operates seamlessly with target hardware.

Security concerns in embedded Linux systems can be particularly acute due to their potential deployment in sensitive environments. From IoT devices to industrial control systems, the risk of attacks showcasing vulnerabilities within the kernel or software applications can compromise system integrity. Ensuring that systems are configured correctly with appropriate security mechanisms—like SELinux or AppArmor—helps protect devices against potential exploits. Additionally, developers must adhere to secure coding practices and conduct thorough testing to identify and rectify vulnerabilities throughout the development lifecycle, ensuring that security is integrated within the entire development process.

Upgrading and maintaining embedded Linux systems also introduce unique challenges. Often, once deployed, these embedded systems may not be accessible for remote maintenance. Developing a strategy for secure and efficient updates, accommodating both software patches and kernel upgrades, becomes essential. Furthermore, developers are often tasked with ensuring that critical updates do not compromise existing functionality, requiring rigorous testing before deployment.

Development environment setup and toolchain selection can pose additional obstacles when transitioning from traditional software development to embedded Linux development. Cross-compilation becomes necessary as developers typically write code on x86 or x64 machines, which must be compiled for the target architecture (such as ARM or MIPS). Understanding cross-compilation toolchains and proper setup is essential for developers aiming to build reliable embedded Linux systems.

Documentation or the lack thereof can also complicate the development process for embedded Linux systems. Often, open-source projects lack comprehensive documentation, leading to confusion among developers trying to utilize disparate components or libraries. Contributing to or establishing clear documentation not only benefits individual developers but can also enhance the collaborative nature of the community and facilitate smoother contributions.

In summary, the field of embedded Linux development is filled with challenges, including resource limitations, real-time requirements, hardware compatibility, security concerns, maintenance strategies, toolchain complexities, and documentation gaps. Embracing these challenges requires a comprehensive understanding of embedded systems, the Linux kernel, and active engagement with the broader community. By leveraging best practices, building tailored solutions, and fostering open dialogue, developers can navigate the hurdles of embedded Linux systems effectively, establishing reliable and robust solutions that enhance the technological landscape. As the demand for embedded Linux systems continues to grow, addressing these challenges will be essential for realizing the full potential of Linux in diverse applications across various industries.

9.5. Case Studies of Real-time Applications

The increasing prevalence of real-time applications in various industries underscores the importance of optimizing performance while meeting strict timing constraints. In the domain of Linux, a versatile platform that can be tailored for real-time operations, several case studies illustrate how developers have effectively leveraged the kernel's capabilities to achieve real-time expectations. These case studies highlight the diversity of applications and the innovative approaches used to tackle unique challenges associated with real-time performance.

One notable case study is that of an autonomous vehicle manufacturer that utilized Linux for its real-time navigation and control systems. This system required precise timing to ensure the vehicle could respond to sensor inputs instantaneously, avoiding potential collisions and navigating complex environments. To achieve this, the development team implemented the PREEMPT-RT patch, transforming the standard Linux kernel into a real-time kernel capable of preempting lower-priority tasks. This allowed critical navigation algorithms to interrupt ongoing processes, ensuring timely responses and maintaining safety.

The project also involved customizing the task scheduling configuration to accommodate the specific requirements of the on-board systems. By assigning higher priorities to time-sensitive tasks and employing real-time scheduling policies (such as FIFO), developers ensured that the navigation software received the CPU time it needed to function optimally. The integration of performance monitoring tools, like `perf`, allowed the team to continuously analyze system latencies and optimize the code for efficiency. Through careful tuning, they achieved the desired real-time performance while incorporating built-in safety checks to mitigate risks.

A second case study revolves around a telecommunications company that employed Linux to manage its network packet processing systems. In this context, the timeliness of packet delivery is crucial for quality of service—especially for VoIP and video streaming applications. By utilizing the Linux kernel's support for Traffic Control (tc) and scheduling classes, the development team implemented advanced queuing disciplines to prioritize network packets based on their urgency.

Further optimizations included the adaptation of CPU affinity settings to bind specific packet processing tasks to dedicated CPU cores, reducing context-switching overhead and improving determinism in response times. The tuning of relevant kernel parameters, such as those controlling network buffer sizes and congestion control mechanisms, allowed the developers to minimize latencies during peak traffic periods. The finely-tuned Linux kernel, informed by extensive profiling and monitoring efforts, delivered robust storytelling experiences for end-users while meeting the demands of contemporary telecommunication services.

In another real-time application case study, a medical imaging system was developed to provide urgent diagnostic capabilities for healthcare professionals. This system needed to process high-resolution images with minimal delay to inform critical medical decisions. By building a custom version of the Linux kernel tailored to the specific hardware used in the imaging devices, developers optimized the underlying system for performance and responsiveness.

Implementing real-time kernel features such as preemptible kernel configurations and configuring scheduling policies allowed the imaging tasks to execute within strict timing requirements. Additionally, emphasis was placed on minimizing unnecessary interrupts and optimizing memory management, ensuring that large image files could be processed efficiently without delay. The testing phases incorporated real-world scenarios, allowing developers to refine the system continuously while focusing on responsiveness and reliability.

A fourth case study reflects a collaborative project among various organizations focused on developing a real-time control system for industrial automation. This project involved the integration of multiple sensor inputs and control algorithms interacting with robotics and conveyor systems. The system required synchronization between sensors, actuators, and data processing components to achieve precise control of industrial processes.

To meet these real-time demands, the team adopted the PREEMPT-RT patch and utilized Linux's real-time capabilities alongside custom kernel modules to manage specific I/O operations. They also developed a robust messaging architecture that allowed different components of the system to communicate efficiently while respecting timing constraints. The implementation of comprehensive logging and monitoring frameworks enabled the team to analyze latencies and intervene proactively to optimize performance.

In each of these case studies, the engineers faced distinct challenges that required creative solutions and collaboration across various disciplines. Optimizing real-time performance involved leveraging the advanced features of the Linux kernel, effectively tuning parameters, and implementing robust testing frameworks. The implementation of real-time features, enabled by the PREEMPT-RT patch and real-time scheduling policy configurations, was pivotal in delivering high-performance systems that met the stringent demands of their respective applications.

Overall, these case studies illustrate the adaptability of the Linux kernel to serve real-time applications across diverse industries. As demand for real-time performance continues to rise, the successful integration of Linux within these systems showcases the power of open-source software to substitute traditional proprietary solutions. Through knowledge-sharing, continuous evolution, and collaborative efforts in kernel development, the Linux community can continue to support and enrich the growing landscape of real-time applications, ultimately contributing to advancements in technology and improving user experiences across various sectors.

10. Open Source Philosophy and Ethics

10.1. The Spirit of Open Source

In the dynamic landscape of technology, the spirit of open source holds a transformative power that inspires collaboration, innovation, and community-driven development. It embodies a philosophy centered around the belief that knowledge, creativity, and tools should be shared freely, allowing all who are interested to participate, learn, and contribute. This principle serves as the bedrock of the Linux ecosystem and has significantly influenced the way software is developed, distributed, and utilized.

At its core, the spirit of open source promotes the idea that software should be accessible to everyone, regardless of their background or financial means. By allowing anyone to view, modify, and distribute the source code, open-source projects empower individuals to take ownership of the technology they interact with. This egalitarian approach shifts the power dynamics in software development, allowing users to become active participants rather than passive consumers. In the case of the Linux kernel, this spirit has fostered a global community of developers who contribute to its evolution, enhancing its capabilities and promoting its adoption across countless devices and applications.

The open-source movement has roots in the early days of computing when collaboration was commonplace among programmers. Sharing code with peers was seen as a way to accelerate learning and foster innovation. The establishment of organizations like the Free Software Foundation (FSF) and the Open Source Initiative (OSI) solidified these ideals, ensuring that open-source principles received formal recognition and support. The ethos championed by notable figures like Richard Stallman and Linus Torvalds set the stage for what would become one of the most successful collaborative endeavors in history.

One of the critical aspects of the spirit of open source is transparency. Open-source projects promote an environment where code reviews, discussions, and contributions happen in public forums, allowing anyone to scrutinize and learn from the work of others. This transparency builds trust within the community, as participants can verify the integrity of the code and the intentions behind it. In contrast to proprietary models that operate in secrecy, open-source development thrives on feedback and public contributions, leading to higher quality and more secure software.

Additionally, the spirit of open source cultivates a culture of shared responsibility. In the Linux community, contributors take pride in the collective achievement of creating robust software capable of powering everything from personal computers to supercomputers and web servers. This shared responsibility extends to various aspects of development, such as security practices, documentation, and user support. Developers actively engage in mentoring newcomers, helping them navigate the complexities of kernel development while encouraging them to contribute their insights and skills.

The flexibility inherent in open-source paradigms also allows developers to customize software to meet specific needs. The Linux kernel exemplifies this adaptability, with thousands of developers contributing to different subsystems, enabling it to run on a wide range of hardware architectures. Whether it's modifying the kernel for a high-performance computing environment or creating a lightweight distribution for embedded devices, the open-source spirit encourages experimentation, resulting in tailored solutions that cater to diverse requirements.

However, alongside the advantages of open-source development, challenges exist. The very openness that fosters innovation can also lead to fragmentation, where multiple variations of software emerge, complicating user experience and support. Additionally, contributors must navigate issues of licensing and compliance, ensuring that their work respects the licensing agreements governing the use and distribution of open-source software. Understanding licensing intricacies becomes vital for developers in the community to promote a responsible and ethical dialogue around contributions.

The impact of open-source philosophy extends beyond the realm of software development; it has implications for society at large. Open-source initiatives have democratized access to technology, enabling individuals and organizations—especially in developing regions—to leverage software tools for education, healthcare, and economic development. This spirit fosters an environment of collaboration that transcends geographical and cultural boundaries, bolstering global efforts towards technological equity.

In the ever-evolving landscape of technology, the spirit of open source remains a guiding force for developers, organizations, and users alike. As the Linux ecosystem continues to flourish under the collaborative efforts of its global community, the principles of transparency, shared responsibility, and innovation coalesce into a potent force for progress. Embracing this spirit will ensure that technology remains accessible, adaptable, and driven by the collective contributions of those who believe in the power of collaboration and open knowledge. It serves not only as a hallmark of the Linux kernel but as a testament to the potential of cooperative endeavors to influence and reshape our digital world for the better.

10.2. Licensing and Legal Issues

In the realm of software development, licensing and legal issues play a critical role in shaping the practices, contributions, and adoption of open-source projects like the Linux kernel. Understanding these complexities is essential for developers, contributors, and organizations looking to leverage the power of Linux while ensuring compliance with legal frameworks and protecting their intellectual property. This subchapter delves into the intricate landscape of licensing, legal considerations, and the implications that arise in the context of kernel development.

At the heart of open-source software is the concept of licensing, which establishes the terms under which the software can be used, modified, and distributed. Various licenses govern open-source projects, each carrying its own stipulations regarding rights and responsibilities. The most widely used license for the Linux kernel is the GNU General Public License (GPL), specifically GPLv2. This license stipulates that any derivative work based on the kernel must also be distributed under the same license. As a result, developers who modify the kernel or create software that links to it must comply with the GPL's requirements, ensuring that their code remains open-source.

The implications of GPL licensing extend beyond mere compliance; they foster a culture of collaboration, shared responsibility, and collective growth within the kernel community. The viral nature of GPL means that contributions made to the Linux kernel benefit all users, allowing enhancements and innovations to propagate freely throughout the ecosystem. This principle not only drives innovation but also provides assurances to contributors that their efforts will not be appropriated for proprietary gain.

However, the legal landscape surrounding licenses can be intricate. Developers must navigate potential complications, such as license compatibility. Not all open-source licenses are compatible with one another; for instance, mixing code governed by GPLv2 with code governed by licenses like the MIT License can lead to legal ambiguities regarding the terms under which the combined work can be distributed. Therefore, developers need to be vigilant when incorporating third-party code into their projects, ensuring that they adhere to licensing stipulations and consider the implications of license compatibility.

In addition to understanding licenses, developers must also be aware of the potential legal ramifications associated with contributions. Code contributions to the Linux kernel imply that developers affirm they possess the rights to the code they submit. This means that developers must avoid incorporating code snippets from proprietary projects or third-party libraries without proper authorization. Infringing on the intellectual property rights of others can lead to legal disputes that jeopardize not only the contributor's reputation but also the stability of the kernel itself.

Moreover, organizations that contribute to the Linux kernel must navigate the intricacies of corporate policy and compliance. Establishing guidelines for developers regarding intellectual property, code submission processes, and legal protections is essential for organizations aiming to participate effectively in the kernel ecosystem. Having clear policies fosters responsibility and ensures that contributions align with broader business goals while adhering to legal obligations.

Another critical consideration in the context of licensing and legal issues is the role of trademarks. The Linux kernel, along with its associated distributions, involves the use of trademarks that are protected by law. The use of names such as "Linux" or "Linux Kernel" in software products or services must comply with trademark regulations and requirements. Misuse of trademarks can result in accusations of misrepresentation, which can undermine trust within the community and have potential legal consequences.

As the Linux kernel continues to evolve and expand, so too will the legal considerations surrounding its development. Ensuring that contributors and organizations are informed about updated licensing practices, legal standards, and emerging trends will be essential in navigating the complexities of open-source development in the future. Engaging in discussions within the kernel community, participating in forums, and networking during conferences can help individuals stay abreast of changes in licensing and legal considerations.

To summarize, navigating the landscape of licensing and legal issues in Linux kernel development requires a thorough understanding of open-source licenses, intellectual property rights, and trademark regulations. The GPL license embodies the philosophy of collaboration and open-source sharing, while the complexities of license compatibility, compliance, and trademark protection demand vigilant consideration. By fostering a culture of awareness and responsibility regarding these legal matters, developers and organizations can contribute meaningfully to the Linux ecosystem while ensuring that their contributions align with the principles of open source and the legal frameworks governing it.

10.3. Open Source Contributions and Etiquette

Open-source contributions and etiquette play a pivotal role in ensuring the success and integrity of projects like the Linux kernel. Understanding the principles of collaboration, communication, and respect is essential for creating a healthy and productive community where innovation thrives and diversity is celebrated. This section explores the nuances of contributing to open-source projects, emphasizing etiquette, best practices, and the impact that a collaborative mindset can have on the broader ecosystem.

First and foremost, it is essential to recognize that open-source contributions are not just about writing code. They encompass a wide range of activities, including documentation, bug reports, testing, and community support. Every contribution, regardless of its size or nature, plays a part in enhancing the project. This inclusivity encourages individuals from diverse backgrounds and skill sets to participate, enriching the community with fresh perspectives and ideas. Thus, contributors should appreciate the value of non-code contributions and actively engage in areas where they can effectively support the project.

Effective communication is another cornerstone of successful open-source contributions. The Linux kernel community primarily relies on mailing lists and forums for discussions and code submissions. When submitting patches or changes, contributors should adhere to clear and concise commit message guidelines, detailing the rationale behind their contributions and referencing pertinent discussions or tickets. Good commit messages not only provide context for reviewers but also serve as an invaluable resource for future contributors seeking to understand the development history and decisions made throughout the project's evolution.

Moreover, contributors should approach discussions and code reviews with an open and respectful attitude. The diverse nature of the open-source community means that contributors come from various backgrounds, cultures, and levels of expertise. It is vital to cultivate an environment where individuals feel comfortable sharing their ideas and asking questions. Adopting a constructive tone when providing feedback, whether it's praise for well-implemented changes or suggestions for improvement, fosters a sense of community and encourages further engagement.

Inclusivity and transparency resonate closely with open-source etiquette. Developers should strive to create an inclusive atmosphere by respecting and encouraging diverse voices within the community. This includes being mindful of language used in discussions, avoiding terminology that may exclude or alienate, and actively supporting initiatives aimed at promoting diversity within the project. Respecting contributors' perspectives—particularly those from underrepresented groups—can lead to collaborative growth and innovation.

It's also crucial to understand the importance of issue tracking and resolving conflicts professionally. When encountering disagreements or differing opinions on technical matters, contributors should engage in discussions focusing on the technical aspects of the problem—or offering potential solutions—rather than resorting to personal attacks or derogatory remarks. Striving for a collaborative spirit and seeking common ground can effectively resolve conflicts while reinforcing a culture of respect and collaboration.

Another essential component of open-source contributions is acknowledgment and attribution. The Linux kernel community greatly values the recognition of contributions, and contributors should take care to appropriately credit and attribute any code, ideas, or work they may have built upon from others. Fostering an environment where contributors feel appreciated for their efforts helps nurture a sense of belonging and loyalty to the community.

Additionally, it is important to approach contributions with a mindset of continuous learning. The open-source community provides an incredible wealth of knowledge through its members, and contributors should actively seek to engage and learn from others. This willingness to learn fosters an environment where people share expertise, refine their skills, and grow as developers—ultimately strengthening the project as a whole.

As one navigates the open-source ecosystem, maintaining ethical integrity is paramount. Contributors should prioritize transparency, accountability, and the responsible use of code. Avoiding copyright infringement, respecting licensing agreements, and ensuring that contributions do not introduce security vulnerabilities or proprietary code aligns with the ethical principles of open-source development. By responsibly managing these aspects, contributors help uphold the sanctity of the project and contribute to its sustainability.

In conclusion, open-source contributions and etiquette form the bedrock of the collaborative spirit that drives innovative projects like the Linux kernel. By adhering to principles of effective communication, respect, inclusion, transparency, and ethical integrity, contributors can foster a positive and productive community environment where ideas can flourish and collaboration can thrive. Each contribution, whether code or otherwise, enriches the open-source ecosystem, and through collective efforts, contributors not only advance their skills but also help propel the next wave of technological innovation. The commitment to open-source etiquette ensures that the kernel community continues to flourish, driving the evolution of technology in a manner that remains accessible and beneficial for all.

10.4. The Impact of Open Source on Society

In recent years, the impact of open source on society has been profound, transforming how we think about software, technology, and collaborative efforts across a multitude of domains. Open source is not just a development model but a movement that fosters community-driven innovation and accessibility, emphasizing the importance of transparency, collaboration, and inclusivity. This subchapter explores the various facets of this impact, focusing on how open source, particularly the Linux kernel and its ecosystem, has reshaped technological landscapes and influenced social dynamics.

One of the most notable impacts of open source is its role in democratizing access to technology. By enabling anyone to access, modify, and distribute software, open source empowers users across socio-economic backgrounds to leverage technology without the constraints typically imposed by proprietary solutions. This democratization has paved the way for innovation, especially in regions where access to technology was previously limited due to licensing fees or restrictive software practices. Schools, startups, and grassroots initiatives can integrate open-source solutions into their projects, fostering creativity and encouraging self-reliance.

The collaborative nature of open-source projects, epitomized by the Linux kernel, has fostered a culture of knowledge-sharing that transcends geographical and cultural barriers. Developers and users from around the globe can contribute ideas, share improvements, and help solve problems collectively. As a result, open-source projects advance more rapidly, leveraging the genius and expertise of diverse individuals who are united by shared goals. This spirit of collaboration not only aids in technical advancement but also builds communities based on shared values and common interests, fostering a sense of belonging among contributors.

Moreover, the influence of open source has reached beyond individual projects, fundamentally reshaping industries. Many organizations adopt open-source software and incorporate open-source principles into their operations, harnessing the collective intelligence of the community to enhance their in-house processes. Companies such as Red Hat, Canonical, and Google have leveraged the power of open source, building businesses around open-source technologies while contributing back to the community. This model establishes a sustainable ecosystem where both the community and industry can thrive, leading to accelerated technology adoption and innovation.

In terms of innovation, the rapid pace at which open-source projects can evolve stands in juxtaposition to the often more constrained development cycles of proprietary software. This agility facilitates experimentation, enabling developers to test out new ideas and roll out updates quickly. The presence of feedback loops within the open-source community further amplifies this dynamic, as users can report issues, suggest features, and contribute code, allowing for continuous improvement of software products. The Linux kernel, with its robust development community, is a prime example of the effectiveness of this model, consistently integrating improvements over time.

However, the impact of open source on society does not come without challenges. The complexity of managing contributions, ensuring quality, and maintaining cohesion within vast communities can sometimes lead to fragmentation. Various forks of popular projects may arise, diverging from the original since contributors pursue different goals or visions. While fostering diversity and innovation, this fragmentation can lead to challenges in interoperability, support, and cohesion within the ecosystem, potentially alienating users or contributors who struggle to keep up with multiple variations.

Additionally, concerns around security frequently surface in discussions of open-source software. The very transparency that fosters collaboration can also expose vulnerabilities, as malicious actors can scrutinize source code for potential exploits. However, the open-source community often proves resilient, with developers working together to patch vulnerabilities rapidly and mitigate threats. Security features integrated into systems like the Linux kernel, such as SELinux and mandatory access controls, exemplify how the community emphasizes the importance of security while adhering to open-source principles.

Of equal importance are the issues surrounding privacy. Open-source projects can serve as a double-edged sword: while they inherently promote user agency and transparency, they can also inadvertently expose sensitive data if not properly managed. Privacy advocates emphasize the need for robust practices in handling user data, tracking how data is collected, stored, and used within projects. Building a culture that prioritizes user privacy is critical to maintaining trust and ensuring that technology benefits society at large.

The educational impact of open source is another significant area of influence. By providing access to source code and documentation, students and aspiring developers can learn valuable skills by examining real-world codebases. This hands-on approach fosters a culture of curiosity and experimentation, encouraging individuals to engage deeply with technology. Many educational institutions incorporate open-source principles into their curricula, preparing the next generation of innovators to thrive in a digital world.

In summary, the impact of open source on society is multifaceted, driving innovation, democratizing access to technology, and fostering collaborative communities. Despite the challenges associated with fragmentation, security vulnerabilities, and privacy concerns, the benefits of open source, particularly as exemplified by the Linux kernel, remain profound. The spirit of open source has not only transformed how software is developed and used but also how communities engage, learn, and innovate collectively. As we continue to navigate the digital age, understanding and supporting the principles of open source will be crucial to shaping a technological landscape that prioritizes accessibility, collaboration, and the shared advancement of society.

10.5. Navigating Open Source Communities

Navigating open source communities effectively is essential for anyone interested in contributing to projects like the Linux kernel. These communities are vibrant, dynamic, and often filled with passionate individuals who share a common goal: to create innovative software solutions that are accessible to all. However, the open source landscape can sometimes feel overwhelming, especially for newcomers. Understanding the culture, communication practices, and norms within these communities is critical to fostering productive interactions, gaining valuable assistance, and becoming an effective contributor.

The first step in navigating open source communities is to familiarize yourself with the project's communication channels. In the case of the Linux kernel, discussions primarily occur through mailing lists, forums, and online repositories like GitHub. The Linux kernel mailing list (LKML) serves as the main forum for technical discussions, patch submissions, and community announcements. Regularly reading the discussions on LKML helps newcomers understand ongoing efforts, opening issues, and the types of contributions being discussed. Engaging in these discussions allows contributors to ask questions and receive feedback from experienced developers.

It's essential to approach communication with clarity and respect. Crafting well-defined messages when seeking assistance or submitting code is vital to garnering positive engagement. When posing questions or providing feedback, clearly outline your thoughts, include pertinent context, and be open to suggestions. This clarity fosters constructive dialogues and ensures that your contributions are valued and understood. Adhering to netiquette—politeness, patience, and consideration for others in online discussions—promotes a positive atmosphere within the community.

Additionally, effective contributions often require reading and understanding established project guidelines. The Linux kernel community has specific coding standards, submission procedures, and review protocols designed to maintain quality and coherence in the codebase. Before contributing a patch, be sure to review the relevant documentation, such as the "SubmittingPatches" document, which details how to format and present your changes for review. Following these guidelines is crucial for effective participation and enhances the chances of your submissions being accepted.

Engagement in collaborative events, such as conferences or hackathons, can provide invaluable opportunities to connect with the community. Events like the Linux Developers Conference bring together developers, maintainers, and enthusiasts from across the globe to share knowledge and work on projects together. Such gatherings foster relationships that can lead to mentorship, collaboration, and deeper involvement in the community.

Within open source communities, mentorship is a structured opportunity for knowledge-sharing that contributes significantly to success. More experienced developers often take the initiative to guide newcomers through the intricacies of coding practices, project philosophies, and collaborative workflows. As a newcomer, don't hesitate to reach out to potential mentors, ask for advice, and express willingness to learn. Conversely, if you are experienced, sharing your expertise and assisting others paves the way for growth within the community.

Another prudent approach is to make use of collaborative tools and resources available to the community. Platforms like GitHub, GitLab, and various project wikis offer valuable information, documentation, and collaborative environments where developers can contribute and track project progress. Participating in these platforms enhances your understanding of the project's structure, ongoing issues, and existing code.

It's also important to respect the intellectual property rights and licensing associated with the project. Open source communities operate on the principles of transparency and sharing, but contributors must remain cognizant of licensure type, ensuring that their contributions align with the project's licensing agreements. Familiarize yourself with the licensing terms to avoid infringing upon rights and to promote a culture of compliance and accountability.

Effective conflict resolution is part of navigating open source communities. Misunderstandings and differences in opinions are common, particularly when discussing technical strategies or design decisions. It's crucial to approach conflicts with composure and a problem-solving mindset. Keeping discussions focused on the issues rather than personal differences allows for constructive resolutions that benefit everyone involved.

Finally, actively participate in the open source ecosystem. Contribute not only through code but also through documentation, bug reports, providing support to others, and engaging in community discussions.

Your participation is key to nurturing the community, making it more inclusive and fostering an environment for shared learning and growth.

In conclusion, successfully navigating open source communities involves understanding communication practices, engaging respectfully, adhering to guidelines, and actively participating in the collaborative ecosystem. By fostering relationships, seeking mentorship, and contributing effectively, you become part of a thriving community dedicated to promoting innovation and shared knowledge in projects like the Linux kernel. Embrace the spirit of collaboration inherent in these communities, and you will not only enhance your skills and knowledge but also leave a lasting impact on the open-source landscape.

11. Security and Privacy in Linux

11.1. Kernel Security Features and Tools

Kernel Security Features and Tools play an indispensable role in the broader landscape of Linux development, establishing vital safeguards that protect both the kernel itself and the systems it governs. As modern computing environments continue to evolve and grow more complex, the sophistication and capabilities of security features and tools within the Linux kernel have likewise advanced, offering comprehensive mechanisms designed to thwart threats and respond to vulnerabilities that could compromise system integrity.

One of the foundational security features embedded within the Linux kernel is the capability for multi-level access controls, with the predominant model being Discretionary Access Control (DAC), augmented by additional frameworks such as Mandatory Access Control (MAC). The traditional DAC permits users to control the permissions of their files and processes; however, it is MAC that provides an additional, robust layer of control. Tools like SELinux (Security-Enhanced Linux) and AppArmor implement MAC by allowing administrators to define strict access policies that govern not only what actions processes can take, but also which resources they can interact with. Through precise security labels and policies, SELinux and AppArmor reduce the risks of privilege escalation and unauthorized resource access, providing a powerful defense against both external threats and internal misconfigurations.

Another crucial security feature of the Linux kernel is its built-in support for cryptography. The kernel includes various cryptographic algorithms and protocols that ensure secure communications over the network, reliable authentication of users and devices, and encryption of sensitive data at rest. By employing these cryptographic features, system administrators can protect critical information and maintain confidentiality, ensuring that unauthorized parties cannot access sensitive data.

The integrity of the kernel and its modules is vital for maintaining overall system security. To this end, kernel module signing features authenticate module code, verifying its integrity and ensuring that only known, trusted modules can be loaded. The system generates a cryptographic signature for approved modules, which the kernel checks during loading. This prevents the introduction of malicious or tampered code that could compromise system stability or security. Consequently, developers involved in kernel module development should follow best practices around signing and manage the associated keys carefully.

Dynamic tracing and monitoring tools, such as `ftrace` and `trace-cmd`, are beneficial for identifying potential security vulnerabilities. These tools enable developers to monitor kernel functions and understand the interactions between them in real time. By providing insights into how the kernel handles specific requests, administrators can glean valuable information about potential attack vectors and system weaknesses, helping to thwart potential exploitation.

Developers can also leverage native kernel debugging tools such as `kgdb`, which offers the ability to debug kernel code during execution. By connecting to another machine (typically through a serial cable), developers can explore kernel states, identify faults, and alter execution paths during crashes—a vital capability for understanding and mitigating security vulnerabilities in real time. Combined with additional tools such as Crash Utility (crash), this functionality becomes invaluable for effective post-mortem analysis of kernel panics and unexpected behavior, allowing developers to respond swiftly and accurately to security weaknesses.

The community-driven nature of Linux further enhances its kernel security landscape. Continuous contributions from developers looking to address security issues, share timely updates, and make improvements ensure that the kernel evolves to meet modern security challenges. Initiatives such as the Kernel Self-Protection Project aim to bolster kernel security through community-driven efforts that promote best practices among developers, enhance awareness, and facilitate discussions surrounding emerging security threats.

One of the distinct advantages of using Linux is the thriving ecosystem of security-focused distributions. Projects such as Tails, Qubes OS, and Kali Linux are designed with security as a foremost priority, leveraging the Linux kernel's security features to create environments optimized for particular use cases, such as anonymity, security testing, or incident response. These distributions integrate tools and features, equipping users and administrators with advanced security settings and functionality tailored to meet specific security requirements.

Furthermore, the pragmatism of open-source development ensures that discoveries related to vulnerabilities can be swiftly communicated and addressed within the community. Disclosures regarding security vulnerabilities lead to collaborative efforts focused on developing patches and mitigation strategies. By maintaining an open dialogue around security, developers and users alike are better equipped to navigate emerging threats and contribute to securing the kernel and its associated components.

In summary, Kernel Security Features and Tools provide a robust framework for protecting the Linux kernel against vulnerabilities and potential exploits. With capabilities such as access control mechanisms, cryptographic support, module signing, dynamic tracing, and a dedicated community that rapidly addresses security issues, Linux has established itself as a resilient platform capable of meeting the security challenges of modern computing environments. By understanding and leveraging these features, developers can contribute to a more secure Linux ecosystem and ensure that systems remain robust against evolving threats in the digital landscape. As the open-source community continues to engage in creative problem-solving and collective security measures, the kernel will undoubtedly remain an enduring and formidable force in the world of technologies.

11.2. Privacy Concerns in Kernel Development

In today's digital age, where data breaches and privacy concerns are increasingly prevalent, the relevance of privacy in kernel development cannot be overstated. The kernel operates at the core of the operating system, managing not only hardware interactions but also data flows, user processes, and system calls. Consequently, any vulnerabilities or flaws in kernel code can have far-reaching implications for system integrity and user privacy. Understanding privacy concerns in kernel development requires an exploration of how the kernel handles data, the threats it faces, and the methodologies necessary for safeguarding user information.

One of the primary challenges in maintaining privacy within the kernel is the handling of sensitive user data. By its nature, the kernel has unrestricted access to all system resources, including personal data. Kernel developers must implement data access policies carefully to ensure that unauthorized processes or users cannot access sensitive information. This includes ensuring that user and process memory spaces are adequately isolated to prevent information leakage between applications.

Moreover, the management of user credentials and authentication adds another layer of complexity to privacy concerns. The kernel acts as a gatekeeper, authenticating users and controlling access to system resources. Any misconfiguration or vulnerability in this process can lead to unauthorized users gaining access to sensitive system areas, compromising user privacy. Implementing robust authentication mechanisms and employing industry-standard practices for password handling, such as hashing and salting, is vital to ensuring that user credentials remain secure.

Another significant aspect of privacy concerns in kernel development is the handling of logs and telemetry data. The kernel generates logs that contain a wealth of information about user actions and system behavior, which, while crucial for troubleshooting and auditing, can inadvertently expose sensitive data if not managed correctly. Developers must be diligent in ensuring that log files do not contain personally identifiable information (PII) or sensitive user data. Implementing log management policies that anonymize data and enforce access controls on log files is essential to mitigating privacy risks.

Kernel developers must also be acutely aware of how the kernel interfaces with user-space applications. As user applications make system calls to interact with the kernel, developers must ensure proper validation and sanitization of those inputs. Poorly validated inputs can lead to vulnerabilities, such as buffer overflows or injection attacks, that may compromise privacy. Adopting secure coding practices and leveraging kernel APIs that enforce input validation can drastically reduce the risk of leading to privacy breaches.

The area of inter-process communication (IPC) is also a focal point for privacy concerns. IPC mechanisms like shared memory and pipes must be handled carefully to prevent unauthorized access to data being exchanged between processes. Enforcing strict access permissions on IPC mechanisms and using capabilities to restrict accessibility can help mitigate the risks associated with leaking sensitive information via unauthorized channels.

In addition, kernel developers must address threats related to malicious code and exploits that can undermine user privacy. Malware targeting kernel vulnerabilities can compromise user data, escalate privileges, and disrupt normal system operation. To protect against these threats, developers should stay informed about emerging vulnerabilities and ensure timely patching of discovered security flaws. The open-source nature of the Linux kernel model allows developers to review, audit, and address potential vulnerabilities collaboratively, fostering a strong security posture.

Educating developers about privacy ethics and legal considerations is another important aspect of promoting privacy in kernel development. Ensuring compliance with various data protection regulations, such as the General Data Protection Regulation (GDPR) and the California Consumer Privacy Act (CCPA), is vital for organizations handling user data. Developers should be cognizant of the data protection principles embedded within these regulations and ensure that the kernel's design accommodates compliance, such as requiring user consent for data processing.

Finally, engaging with the Linux community can provide additional insights into best practices around privacy in kernel development. By participating in discussions, employing peer reviews, and sharing experiences around privacy concerns, developers can collectively enhance their understanding of the implications of their work on user privacy. This collaborative spirit is essential for fostering an environment where privacy is prioritized, and contributors can learn from each other to create secure and private systems.

In summary, privacy concerns in kernel development are multifaceted, encompassing how the kernel manages user data, authentication, logging, inter-process communication, and the prevention of malicious attacks. By adhering to secure coding practices, implementing robust access controls, staying informed about emerging threats, and considering privacy regulations, kernel developers can play a pivotal role in safeguarding user privacy. The collaborative nature of the Linux kernel community further enriches this endeavor, ensuring that knowledge and best practices surrounding privacy remain central to the kernel's ongoing development.

11.3. Mitigating Security Vulnerabilities

Mitigating security vulnerabilities within the Linux kernel is a critical task for developers and system administrators alike. The kernel is the core component of an operating system, managing communication between hardware and software resources. Given its foundational role, any vulnerabilities in the kernel can lead to serious security risks, potentially compromising data integrity, user privacy, and overall system stability. Therefore, understanding how to effectively mitigate these vulnerabilities is paramount for maintaining a secure computing environment.

One of the first steps in mitigating security vulnerabilities is conducting a comprehensive security audit of the kernel. This involves systematically reviewing the kernel codebase to identify potential weaknesses and coding errors. A thorough security audit can uncover issues such as improper memory management, race conditions, and insufficient input validation—all of which can be exploited by malicious actors. Tools like static analysis software can assist in identifying common patterns associated with vulnerabilities, allowing developers to address these issues proactively.

In addition to audits, maintaining up-to-date knowledge of known vulnerabilities is essential for vulnerability mitigation. Following databases such as the Common Vulnerabilities and Exposures (CVE) list and the National Vulnerability Database (NVD) provides insights into emerging threats. Developers should prioritize patch management by promptly applying security updates and patches released by the kernel community. This practice is critical for protecting systems from exploits that may target known vulnerabilities. It is advisable to implement automated patch management solutions or establish routine manual checks to ensure that systems are always running the most secure versions available.

A significant feature for mitigating security vulnerabilities in the kernel is the implementation of Mandatory Access Control (MAC) systems such as SELinux (Security-Enhanced Linux) or AppArmor. These security modules provide additional layers of control compared to traditional Discretionary Access Control (DAC). By defining strict policies that govern how processes interact with user files and resources, administrators can limit the potential impact of any security vulnerabilities. MAC systems effectively reduce the attack surface, as even if an exploit occurs within a process, the extent of its capabilities can be restricted by the security policies in place.

Another powerful mechanism for mitigating vulnerabilities is the use of kernel configuration options that enhance security during kernel compilation. For example, enabling stack protection features, such as stack canaries, can thwart certain types of buffer overflow attacks. Similarly, Address Space Layout Randomization (ASLR) can be configured to prevent attackers from predicting the locations in memory where key functions reside, further complicating exploit attempts. Collectively, these compile-time options contribute to a kernel more resistant to common attack vectors.

Isolation of critical components is another effective technique for minimizing the potential for security breaches. In systems where security is paramount, using virtualization or containerization technologies to isolate processes can prevent security vulnerabilities from affecting the entire system. This approach limits the damage a compromised component can inflict and allows for more stringent access controls to be enforced in sensitive environments.

Additionally, regular penetration testing and vulnerability assessments should be an integral part of a security strategy. By simulating real-world attacks on the kernel and associated applications, organizations can identify weaknesses before they are exploited. These assessments provide direct feedback on how well existing security measures are performing and help inform the ongoing development of security strategies.

Education and awareness within the development community are also critical for mitigating vulnerabilities. By fostering a security-conscious culture, developers can become more vigilant in recognizing potential issues and developing secure coding practices. Engaging in discussions, attending workshops, and participating in security-focused initiatives can help promote this culture and equip developers with the tools and knowledge necessary for secure kernel development.

Lastly, leveraging community wisdom within the Linux kernel ecosystem is invaluable. The open-source community prides itself on transparency and collaborative problem-solving. Contributing to or participating in discussions on mailing lists or forums allows developers to share real-time information about vulnerabilities, mitigation strategies, and security best practices. Internalizing the lessons learned from previous vulnerabilities can help fortify the kernel against future threats.

In summary, mitigating security vulnerabilities in the Linux kernel entails a combination of proactive measures, such as conducting thorough audits and maintaining up-to-date knowledge of security issues, along with implementing robust access control mechanisms and leveraging community resources. By adhering to security best practices throughout the kernel development process, developers can help create a more secure operating environment, protecting user data and maintaining the integrity of Linux-based systems. The continuous evolution of threats underscores the importance of these measures, as vigilance and collaboration within the kernel community remain critical to ensuring future security.

11.4. Security-focused Kernel Distros

Security-focused Linux distributions, often referred to as "security-focused kernel distros," have been designed with the primary goal of enhancing the security posture of the systems they run on. These distributions leverage the foundational strengths of the Linux kernel and its security features while incorporating specialized tools and configurations aimed specifically at threat mitigation, secure communications, data protection, and user privacy. Understanding the attributes and advantages of these security-focused distros is essential for anyone seeking to deploy Linux in environments where security is paramount.

One of the foremost examples of a security-focused distro is Qubes OS, which adopts a unique approach to security through isolation and virtualization. Qubes OS utilizes Xen-based virtualization to compartmentalize applications and services into isolated qubes, or lightweight virtual machines. By segregating different tasks into their own controlled environments, even if one qube is compromised, the attacker is limited in capability and cannot easily access or affect other qubes. This architecture fundamentally changes the risk landscape, allowing users to run potentially unsafe applications alongside sensitive operations without compromising the integrity of their data.

Another well-known example is Tails, a live operating system designed for privacy and anonymity. Tails runs entirely from RAM, ensuring that all traces of user activity are wiped from the system upon shutdown. It utilizes the Tor network to anonymize user internet traffic, making it challenging for entities to track the user's online activity. Tails is particularly valuable for individuals operating in compromised environments or those needing to ensure that their activities remain confidential. The development of Tails underscores the principle of minimizing data retention and enhancing user privacy—a crucial aspect of security-focused distros.

Kali Linux is another prominent security-focused distribution, tailored for penetration testing and security auditing. By pre-packaging a vast array of security tools, Kali allows security professionals and ethical hackers to perform vulnerability assessments, penetration tests, and forensic analysis more effectively. The kernel of Kali is configured to enable these tools to work effectively, with particular attention given to features like network packet injection, which are essential for testing wireless security. By providing a comprehensive suite of tools, Kali enables security professionals to proactively identify and address vulnerabilities within systems.

Additionally, a key feature of security-focused Linux distros is the emphasis on robust access control mechanisms. For instance, distributions like SELinux or Fedora (which includes SELinux by default) focus on implementing Mandatory Access Control (MAC) policies designed to enforce security at the kernel level. These mechanisms define what each process can access, significantly limiting the impact of security breaches. The proven efficacy of SELinux in securing systems beyond standard Discretionary Access Control (DAC) exemplifies the effectiveness of such tools within security-focused distributions.

Security-focused distros often come with hardened kernels that include custom configurations, patches, and security enhancements. By implementing the latest security best practices, developers can reduce the attack surface area and increase the effectiveness of the system against potential vulnerabilities. These enhancements might include disabling unnecessary services, configuring secure networking options, and instituting strict file permissions—all aimed at minimizing potential entry points for attacks.

In addition to built-in tools and configurations, many security-focused distros prioritize regular updates and patch management. Promptly applying security updates ensures that system vulnerabilities are addressed, which is essential for maintaining a robust defense structure. The communities surrounding these distributions generally emphasize security awareness, encouraging users to stay informed of potential vulnerabilities and the latest security practices.

Collaboration between security-focused distros and broader open-source communities ensures a proactive approach to emerging threats. By sharing findings, reporting vulnerabilities, and working collectively on security enhancements, developers can continuously improve their distros. This commitment to collaboration underpins the open-source ethos, demonstrating that the security of systems is enhanced when knowledge and expertise are shared across communities.

Finally, the emphasis on documentation and educational resources within security-focused distros is integral to user empowerment. By providing comprehensive guides on secure usage, configuration best practices, and common pitfalls to avoid, these distributions equip users with the knowledge necessary to secure their systems effectively.

In conclusion, security-focused kernel distros emerge as essential tools for enhancing the security and privacy of Linux systems. They leverage the capabilities of the Linux kernel while incorporating sophisticated access control mechanisms, hardening techniques, and an array of security tools tailored to meet the demands of sensitive environments. As the landscape of threats evolves, these distributions exemplify the commitment of the Linux community to fostering security, collaboration, and resilience in an increasingly interconnected world. Through understanding and utilizing these security-focused distros, organizations and individuals can significantly strengthen their defenses against potential vulnerabilities, safeguarding their data and enhancing their overall technological integrity.

11.5. Developing for Secure Systems

In today's interconnected digital landscape, the need for secure systems has never been more crucial. With the rise of sophisticated cyber threats, organizations must prioritize the security of their operating systems, applications, and data. The Linux kernel, renowned for its versatility and performance, provides a foundation upon which developers can build secure systems. This subchapter will explore the principles of developing for secure systems with the Linux kernel, emphasizing best practices, tools, and methodologies that can be employed to safeguard systems against vulnerabilities and attacks.

Before embarking on secure development within the Linux kernel, it is essential to understand the fundamental security principles that should guide your practices. The principle of least privilege is paramount; it dictates that code and processes should only have the permissions necessary to perform their assigned tasks. Adhering to this principle minimizes the potential damage caused by security breaches or vulnerabilities. Whenever possible, processes should run with limited privileges, and developers should utilize mechanisms such as user namespaces to provide isolated environments for processes.

In addition to limiting privileges, developers need to adopt a secure coding mindset when writing kernel code. Following predefined coding standards and practices significantly reduces the likelihood of introducing vulnerabilities inadvertently. It is crucial to understand common security threats, such as buffer overflows, race conditions, and improper input validation, as these are prevalent issues in kernel development. Developers should actively implement techniques to sanitize inputs, validate parameters, and manage memory effectively to avert potential exploits.

Using static analysis tools can aid in identifying vulnerabilities during the development phase. Tools such as 'cppcheck,' 'Clang Static Analyzer,' and 'Coverity' can analyze kernel code and identify potential security flaws before they become a liability. Implementing these tools into the development workflow allows for early detection of issues related to coding best practices, leading to improved security.

In addition to static analysis, developers should leverage dynamic testing methods, such as fuzz testing, to uncover vulnerabilities in the kernel. Fuzz testing involves feeding randomly generated data to the system to identify unexpected behavior or crashes. This approach can unveil issues that may not be apparent during standard testing, enabling developers to address potential security loopholes proactively.

Another essential aspect of developing secure systems involves configuring the Linux kernel to incorporate security-focused features and patches. Enabling key security configurations—such as stack canaries, position-independent executables (PIE), Address Space Layout Randomization (ASLR), and control flow integrity—significantly enhances resilience against attacks such as code injection and exploitation. Leveraging existing kernel security modules like SELinux or AppArmor provides an additional layer of access control that helps enforce mandatory security policies on processes, files, and networks.

When developing for secure systems, security review processes should be instituted as a commitment to quality assurance. Engaging in code reviews with an emphasis on security-related issues encourages collaborative development efforts and harnesses the wisdom of experienced developers within the community. Cultivating a culture of security thoroughness further amplifies the effectiveness of the kernel development process, ensuring that potential vulnerabilities are monitored and addressed continually.

Effective logging and monitoring practices should also be implemented within the kernel to facilitate real-time detection of suspicious activities and ensure system integrity. By logging critical actions and using tools designed for log analysis, developers can gain insights into the behavior of kernel code and promptly react to anomalies that may indicate security breaches.

Furthermore, a focus on comprehensive documentation is crucial when developing for secure systems. Documenting security features, coding practices, configurations, and potential vulnerabilities is invaluable not only for individual developers but also for future contributors. Clear documentation establishes a shared understanding of security requirements, challenges, and strategies and exemplifies a commitment to transparency within the community.

As organizations embrace the necessity of secure systems, continuous learning and adaptation to new security trends are paramount. Attending workshops, security conferences, and engaging with the broader security community provide avenues for knowledge exchange and deeper insights into emerging threats and best practices.

In conclusion, developing for secure systems within the Linux kernel involves a multifaceted approach that combines adhering to security principles, implementing secure coding practices, utilizing analysis and testing tools, configuring security features, engaging in thorough code reviews, monitoring system behaviors, and maintaining comprehensive documentation. By fostering a culture of security within the kernel community, developers can bolster the integrity and resilience of Linux systems against evolving threats. With vigilance and commitment to security, the Linux kernel can continue to be a reliable foundation for the diverse and dynamic digital landscape that defines the contemporary computing ecosystem.